PHARAOH

Build A Kingdom. Rule The Nile.
Live Forever.™

Credits

Designer	Chris Beatrice
Producers	Greg Sheppard Ken Parker
Director of Technology	Mike Gingerich
Art Director	Darrin Horbal
Programmers	Jason Benham Jim Solomon Gabe Farris Chris Gurski Scott Delekta
Lead Artist	Heidi Mann
Lead Animator	Mike Malone
Artists	Dennis Rose Andrea Muzeroll Bob Curtis Brian Despain Kate Saparoff Ron Alpert Adam Carriuolo
Music	Keith Zizza Henry Beckett

Sound	Ed Saltzman
Writer	Lisa Gagnon
Additional Design	Doug Gonya
	Tony Leier
Quality Assurance Manager	Jon Payne
Lead Tester	Tony Leier
Testers	Clay Heaton
	Chris Bold
	Chris Dixon
	Hans Wang
	John McAuley
	Wayne McCaul
	Brett Levin
Scenario Creators	Clay Heaton
	Tony Leier
	Brett Levin
	John McAuley
	Wayne McCaul
	Ken Parker
	Jon Payne
	Greg Sheppard

Table of Contents

Egypt Welcomes You

Standing on the hot, arid sand, you look towards the little settlement that you call home. In the background, the mighty Nile flows by, and along its muddy banks all manner of vegetation grows, even some small farms that some in your city have planted. Your family has lived and died along the river for generations, ekeing out an existence from what the land has to offer.

Yet, change is in the hot, arid air. A charismatic leader has arisen. His dream is first to unite all the settlements in the region, and then unite all of Egypt. As you ponder this dream, you have a vision: a thriving city stretches out before you. Abundant farms feed a hungry citizenry. Thousands tend to their daily tasks — protecting the city, ensuring its wealth, educating its youth, worshipping its gods, tending to its dead. The voices of your people float in the breeze and reverberate through the streets.

Inspired by your vision, you commit yourself to helping achieve the dream of a united Egypt. You instill in your children the magic of the vision, for you know it may take generations to achieve.

To realize your vision, you must learn the intricacies of the Nile. The Nile is the source of life in Egypt, and its floods bring renewal to the land every year. Learn to manage these floods, and you will make the most of this indispensable resource.

Some basic skills will help you achieve your dream. Some of them may be learned through reading the following pages; others you will have to discover for yourself.

May the gods smile upon you as you proceed along your way!

A Quick Historical Note

The action in *Pharaoh* takes place roughly between 3,200 BC and 1,300 BC. While *Pharaoh* is not a strictly historical game, events in ancient Egyptian history do shape its structure. Refer to the Appendix 2: A brief history of Egypt, starting on page 235, to learn a little about the history of ancient Egypt and to understand the context for some of the events in the game.

A Note on Usage

Throughout this text, you'll see the word "info-click" used. Info-click means different things to different people. For PC users, info-click means right-click (click your right mouse button). For Mac users, info-click means command-click (click your mouse button while holding down the command key). If you are a Mac user with a two-button mouse, info-click still means command-click, unless you map the right mouse button to the command key.

Traveler's Journal

As we were researching ancient Egypt, we found a rare papyrus containing a journal written by an ancient merchant who traveled to Egypt. The journal is excerpted throughout this manual in gray boxes, like the one on the facing page.

Arriving in Egypt
Ahket, 12th year of Ramesses
Morning
Dear Journal,

    My first trip to Egypt —
and as we sailed up the Nile I knew one
thing for certain: I wasn't in Syria anymore.
The Nile itself is unlike any river I've ever
seen. The first thing I noticed was the
refreshingly cool breeze blowing from the
north, cutting through the heat of the day.
The captain of the boat, who had been to
Egypt before on trade missions, told me that
the locals call this breeze the Breath of Ra.

    The captain certainly knew how to
steer the ship. He successfully guided us
through the moving maze that is the Nile.
Trade ships, much like our own, clog the
waterway bringing their bounty from exotic
locales. Fishing boats hauling in the day's
catch made their way to the docks, and
small rafts piloted by local citizens darted
between the larger vessels. Peals of laughter
poured out from a luxury yacht, where some
of the city's wealthiest residents were enjoy-
ing a pleasant cruise. Ferries conveyed peo-
ple, animals and goods from one side of the
river to the other. Crocodiles and hip-
popotamuses
patrolled the
river, looking
for a meal.
The captain
adeptly
maneuvered
our boat
through all
these obstacles
until we final-
ly reached our
destination:
Waset.

Getting Started

Installing *Pharaoh* on the PC

With Windows running on your computer, place the *Pharaoh* CD into your CD-ROM drive. In a few seconds, Windows' AutoPlay feature should display a screen with four buttons: Play, Install, Uninstall and Quit. Click "Install" to begin.

Should AutoPlay not work on your computer, double click (click twice quickly) on the "My Computer" icon on your desktop. Find the icon for your CD-ROM drive and double-click on it. In the menu that appears, find the item called "Setup.exe." Double click on it to start the installation.

The Install program then automatically chooses a file path for *Pharaoh*. If you want to designate your own path for *Pharaoh*, click "Browse" and pick a location. Otherwise, click "Next" to continue the installation.

You'll be asked to choose among Small, Medium and Large Installs. Each version offers the full features of the game; the difference will be the speed of the game. The Full Install puts the entire game on your hard drive. It takes up the most room, but offers the best performance. Laptop users will especially appreciate the ability to remove the CD after the initial copy-protection check. The Medium Install puts the most commonly used elements on your hard drive and takes up less room on your hard drive than the Large Install. The Small Install puts only basic elements on your hard drive and runs the rest of the game's features from the CD. It takes up the least room on your hard drive.

Installing *Pharaoh* can take as long as ten minutes. Once the program is installed, you will see a box detailing the additions *Pharaoh* made to your start menu. *Pharaoh* also offers you the option of adding bookmarks to your internet browser.

At this point, you have the option of reading the "Readme" file. We know you can't wait to see what Egypt holds for you, but we do highly recommend reading this file before you start to play the game. This manual went to print several weeks before the game was finished, and any last minute changes are described in Readme. Anytime this manual is in conflict with Readme, Readme is correct.

Now, click the "Finish" button. If necessary, Install will update some system components. It then might restart your computer.

Starting the Game on the PC

Now that the game is installed, you can start the game in one of two ways:

1. Insert the *Pharaoh* CD into your CD-ROM drive. When the AutoPlay window opens, click the "Play" button.

2. From your start menu, find the Sierra sub-directory and choose *Pharaoh*.

PLEASE NOTE: You must have the *Pharaoh* CD in your CD-ROM drive to start the game. If you chose the Full Install, you may remove the CD after the game begins.

Installing the Game on the Mac

First, place the *Pharaoh* CD into your CD-ROM drive. Double-click on the icon that appears on your desktop. In the window that pops up, double click on the "Pharaoh Installer" icon. Choose the Small, Medium or Full installation (click on each to see how much disk space it requires). Click on your choice and, holding down your mouse button, "drag" the icon to a location displayed in the right-hand panel.

The Small install runs most of the game's sounds and videos from the game CD. Choose this if you have limited space on your hard drive. The Medium install places the most commonly used media files on your hard disk. The Full install puts the entire game on your hard disk for optimum performance.

Starting the Game on the Mac

When your Macintosh finishes transferring files from the CD to your hard disk, double-click on the folder you just created. Inside, you'll find a *Pharaoh* icon. Double-click this icon to start the game. You might want to drag this icon to your computer's desktop to conveniently start the game later.

After Pharaoh Launches

Once you launch the game, a brief movie describing the glory of ancient Egypt plays, followed by credits and the *Pharaoh* title screen. Click on the title screen, and the Main Menu appears.

From here, you can play *Pharaoh*, see which families are deemed to be the Greatest Families, visit the *Pharaoh* web site, or quit the game.

Your Family

When you choose "Play *Pharaoh*," a Family Registry screen appears. The registry lists all the families that have begun to make their mark in history.

To begin a new game of *Pharaoh*, found a new family. From the Registry screen, click on "Create Family." Type in a surname of your choice, or choose from the list of authentic Egyptian names.

Now, you are ready to make your way through Egypt's history. After you have chosen a family name, click "Proceed." From the Choose Game screen that appears, click "Begin Family History." Then, a screen appears which lists the Periods of Egyptian history. Select the first Period, the Pre-Dynastic, then click the button in the lower right of the screen to begin your family's quest.

Continuing History

If you don't play the game all the way through the first time (who needs to sleep or eat?), you can pick up where you left off later. When you are ready to take a break, choose "Save Game" from the File Menu. The next time you start *Pharaoh*, choose your family's name from the

Registry Screen. After you do, the Choose Game screen appears. Click "Continue History" to resume your family's story.

If you forget to save your game before quitting to take a break, don't fret. *Pharaoh* automatically saves your game twice per game year, in January and July. You might lose some of your more recent history, but not all will be lost. Choose "Load Saved Game" from the Choose Game screen and select "autosave_history.sav" to pick up reasonably close to where you left off.

Missions and Mission Briefings

The path leading a united Egypt — and your family — to greatness is a long one with many steps along the way. In *Pharaoh*, these steps are called missions.

At the start of each mission, a Mission Briefing panel describes what you should expect and what you'll need to do. When you meet the goals outlined in the Mission Briefing, you win the mission and move on to the next step.

Missions are grouped into Periods. When you finish the last mission in a Period, you automatically return to the screen that lists all the Periods in Egyptian history. You have to play the Periods chronologically (no fair skipping ahead), but you can click on any of the Periods for a brief description.

Setting a Difficulty Level

Set the level of difficulty at which you'd like to play each mission from the Mission Briefing panel. You can choose from five difficulty levels, spanning the spectrum between "Very Easy" and "Very Hard." You can change your difficulty level at any time during a mission through the Options menu on the Menu Bar. Keep in mind, though, that lowering your difficulty decreases your score (see page 19).

Your Place in the World

It would be difficult to help build and sustain a united Egypt if you ignored other cities in the world. From time to time, other cities, and sometimes even Pharaoh, will request your aid. Generally, they ask for goods or for the services of your military. To foster

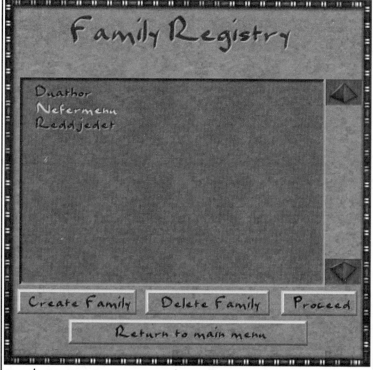

Family Registry Screen. From this screen, you can continue a previous game or start a new one by establishing a new family. If you choose, you can also delete a family. Deleting a family erases all the saved games and any history associated with it.

good relations with your neighbors, you should fulfill these requests if you can. Your reputation will likely increase (see Kingdom Rating, page 194), and Egypt will be stronger for it.

Losing the Game

Even families with the noblest of intentions can meet with ignominious defeat. If you are attacked by a military force stronger than your own, you will most likely lose the game. Sometimes, your city will be attacked through no fault of your own. The invading force might just have their own vision for empire and greatness. You can, though, trigger an attack by your actions or inactions. For example, if you repeatedly ignore requests for aid, a neighboring city or Pharaoh may decide to forcibly take what you would not willingly give.

Gross mismanagement of funds, too, usually means disaster. Going into debt damages your reputation (see Kingdom Rating, page 194), and another city's army or navy may take over your city to demonstrate the Kingdom's disgust with you.

Scoring

At the end of each mission, you are given a score based on how quickly you completed the mission, your ratings, the size of your population, the amount of money in your coffers, the monuments you completed and your difficulty level. If you change your difficulty level during a mission, the lowest difficulty level you played is the one used to figure your score. Your score is recorded for posterity and compared to the scores of other players or yourself. If you have the high score for a particular mission, your family name and final score is displayed in the Greatest Families screen, accessible from the Main Menu.

Other Options

If you need to take a break from the rigors of leading your family through history, Pharaoh offers you a couple of other ways to get a taste of Egypt. These are:

Relive History.   To look back on all you have achieved, choose "Relive History" from the Choose Game screen. Here, your achievements are recorded and celebrated.

You can also replay a completed Mission or an entire completed Period by choosing "Relive History." While you can replay history, you cannot change it. Replaying any missions has no effect on your current full history game.

Please Note: If you are replaying a particular Mission, be sure to save it with a distinct and different name than your full history game. If you accidentally give the Mission the same name as your full game, your history will be overwritten and lost.

If you are replaying a completed mission and forget to save it, open the "autosave" file listed when you choose "Load Saved Game" from the Choose Game screen. Pharaoh automatically saves your mission every six game months, so you'll be able to recover a reasonably up-to-date version of your current mission.

Custom Missions. *Pharaoh* comes with a few missions that are not part of any larger game. To play one of these missions, choose "Custom Missions" from the Choose Game screen. Custom missions are also automatically saved every six game months should you forget to do so yourself.

In-Game Help

Just about everything you need to know about *Pharaoh* is contained right in the game. The "Help" drop-down list in the Menu Bar provides access to detailed information regarding *Pharaoh*.

Mouse help describes some items. If you hold the mouse over Control Panel buttons or Menu Bar items, a small panel briefly describing the object will pop up.

Also, info-clicking on just about anything provides a wealth of information. The first screen that pops up when you info-click an object provides brief information needed to manage your city. The lower left corner of these screens has a question mark. Click on that question mark for a more detailed description of the object and to learn more about the object's role in the game. These entries are usually linked to other useful topics and to historical information. Linked topics are displayed in a different color from the rest of the text.

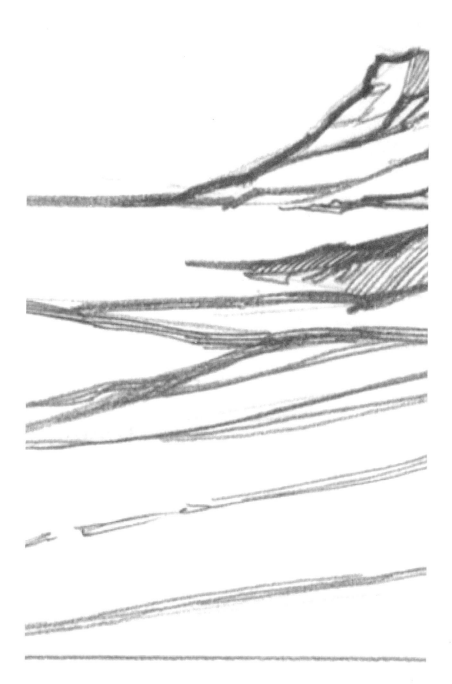

Playing *Pharaoh*

Empty land can be inspiring. With an expanse of land stretching out before you, anything is possible. You can envision the perfect city with majestic temples reaching towards the sky, busy thoroughfares crowded with people and animals, and farmland heavy with crops. Luckily, you have the unique ability to make this perfect city real. The tools described below will help you achieve your dream.

The Control Panel

The Control Panel is your command center: every order you can give in the game can be accessed here.

The Control Panel

When you first begin to play *Pharaoh*, not all the commands on the control panel are available to you. Early in the game, Egypt is a fledgling culture that has not developed fully. As Egyptian culture and civilization evolve, you will be able to build more elaborate cities with more buildings and services for your citizens. Options currently not available are darkened.

You should also note that Egypt's various regions each have different natural resources and landscapes. Some regions are arid, with rich mineral resources, while other regions are lush. Because of this variety and the gradual development of Egyptian culture, the buildings available to you in each mission are different.

Each button on the Control Panel is described below:

Overlay Selector. Click the overlay selector button to choose special, informative views of your city. For more on overlays, see pages 203-209.

Hide Control Panel. Click this button to hide the Control Panel. You'll see more of your city, and you'll still be able to see the building construction buttons, but you won't see the Overview Map or the buttons to access the World Map or the Overseers.

Overview Map. The overview map shows more of your city at one time. Point and click on any part of the map to jump your view to that area. The buildings on the map are color-coded depending on their function. For more on color coding, see page 209.

Overseers Button. Click this button to consult your Overseers. For more on Overseers and their functions within the game, see pages 197-203.

World Map Button. Click this button to view a map of the entire known world. Other cities in the world are clearly marked, and you can watch armies and navies as they make their journeys. For more on the World Map, see page 210.

Housing Button. Click this button to designate housing areas. For more on building housing areas, see pages 40-43.

 Roads Button. Click on this button to build roads. For more on roads, see page 40.

Clear Land Button. Use this button to clear land of obstructions. A special "Dig" cursor appears after you click the button. To read more on clearing land, turn to page 38.

Food and Farming Structures Button. Click this button to build the structures that produce food for your city. Also listed here are farms that grow raw materials for industries. The food and farming structures are Farms, Work Camps, Hunting Lodges, Fishing Wharves, Cattle Ranches, Water Lifts and Irrigation Ditches. For more on food and farming, consult pages 59-67.

Industrial Structures Button. Click here to build any of the industry buildings in *Pharaoh*, including raw material producers, manufacturers and construction guilds. For more on industry in *Pharaoh*, see pages 69-79. For more on construction guilds, see page 130.

Storage and Distribution Structures Button. Click on this button to build a Storage Yard, Granary, Bazaar or Dock. Each structure plays a distinct role in getting goods and food to the city's people. Docks and Storage Yards are also key to trade. For more on distribution of food and goods to citizens, see pages 81-91. For more on trade, go to pages 91-95.

Entertainment Structures Button. When citizens demand entertainment, click this button to build them the attractions they desire, such as Booths, Bandstands, Pavilions and Senet Houses. Use this button to build performers' training facilities as well. For more on entertainment in your city, turn to page 159.

Religious Structures Button. Click here to build Shrines, Temples and a Festival Square. If you are building monuments (like a Pyramid or Sphinx), they will be listed here. For more on religion, consult pages 117-127. More on monuments can be found on pages 129-149.

Education Structures Button. When you are ready to bring the light of learning to the city's well-to-do residents, click the "Education Structures" button and choose either Scribal School or Library. For more on the construction of these two buildings, see pages 165-166.

Health and Sanitation Structures Button. Click on this button to build Wells, Water Supplies, Physician's offices, Mortuaries, Dentist's offices and Apothecaries. For more on Health and Sanitation in *Pharaoh*, visit pages 151-157.

Municipal Structures Button. Clicking this button reveals a long list of buildings that help to keep the city running. Included in the list are the Police Station, Firehouse, Architect's post, Tax Collector's office, Courthouse, Palace, Mansion, Water Crossings, Roadblock and Beautification structures. For more on municipal functions, consult pages 97-115.

Military Structures Button. Click here to begin establishing an army and a navy or to build defensive structures. Buildings listed here include Recruiter, Forts, Academy, Warship Wharf, Transport Wharf, Weaponsmith, Chariot Maker, Wall, Tower and Gatehouse. For more on the military, turn to pages 169-189.

Undo Button. When this button is lit, you can undo your last action. You can undo most actions, but you have only a limited time in which to do so.

Messages Button. Click here to read your messages, including any special instructional messages, which are each marked by a blue scroll. Messages are discussed on page 211.

Trouble Spots Icon. Click here to visit the sites of recent or on-going trouble, such as a fire or building collapse.

Review Assignment Icon. Click this button if you need to refresh your memory regarding your goals for the current mission. See page 17 for more on your mission assignments.

The Menu Bar

The Menu Bar which runs across the top of the screen helps you manage your game play. Under the File Menu, you'll find basic options like loading and saving games. Under Options, you can customize the appearance of the game. The Help Menu is also in the Menu Bar. Should you want to consult a specific Overseer, the Overseers Menu lists each one, and you can choose which you'd like to visit.

Next to the Overseers Menu is the amount of money the city has and its current population size. Next to the population figure is a pyramid. Use this pyramid to reorient your view of the city. Clicking on the right side of the pyramid rotates the city counter-clockwise. Clicking on the left side of the pyramid rotates the city clockwise. Click on the center of the pyramid to reorient your view due north. Rotating your view can be helpful, especially if large buildings obscure your view of structures behind it. The last item on the Menu Bar is the current date.

Keyboard Controls

Pharaoh offers many optional control shortcuts that you can access with a simple keystroke. Please refer to the "Readme" file in your computer's *Pharaoh* folder for any changes or updates to this list.

Key	Effect
A	Orders a selected warship to attack all enemies.
C	Shows the Risks: Crime Overlay, or orders a selected charioteer company to charge.

D   Shows the Risks: Damage Overlay.

E   Orders a selected transport ship to evade enemies.

F   Shows the Risks: Fire Overlay, or orders a selected company to return to its Fort.

H   Orders a selected ship to hold its current position.

L   Centers your view on a different military company each time it's pressed.

         If a company is selected, "L" issues the "hold ground in loose formation" order.

M   When you select a monument from the building list, its image attaches to your cursor and shows you how much land the monument will occupy. Pressing the "M" key freezes the monument's "footprint" into place so that you can move your viewpoint around the city without moving the monument's tentative location. Press the "M" key again to resume normal mouse behavior, or click to place the monument in the footprint's current location.

         Pressing "M" when a military company is selected issues the mop-up order.

N   Orders a selected company or warship to attack nearby enemies.

P   Pauses the flow of time in the game. You cannot build while time is paused.

R   When placing a Statue, Gatehouse or Temple Complex, "R" rotates the structure's orientation one-quarter turn clockwise. Statues will display multiple styles.

           With a military company selected, "R" orders the soldiers to change their orientation (rotate). "R" also orders a selected transport or warship to return to the Shipwright for repairs.

T   Shows the Risks: Problems Overlay.

           With a military company selected, "T" issues the "hold ground in tight formation" order.

W   Shows the Water Overlay.

           If a warship or transport ship is selected, "W" orders the ship to return to its home Wharf.

Space   Press the spacebar to toggle between your last selected Overlay and the normal city view.

Esc   (escape) exits the game.

[(open bracket) reduces game speed by 10 percent.

]   (close bracket) increases game speed by 10 percent.

'   (apostrophe) Overseer of the Workers

1	Overseer of the Military
2	Political Overseer
3	Ratings Overseer
4	Overseer of Commerce
5	Overseer of the Granaries
6	Overseer of Public Health
7	Overseer of Learning
8	Overseer of Diversions
9	Overseer of the Temples
0	Overseer of the Treasury
–	(minus sign) Chief Overseer
=	(equals sign) Overseer of Monuments
F7	Set 640x480 screen resolution
F8	Set 800x600 screen resolution
F9	Set 1024x768 screen resolution

For Players of *Caesar III*

Egypt and Rome are very different places. Some of the skills you learned as a successful Roman Governor may not help you as an Egyptian Leader. If you are a fan of

Caesar III, take note of of the following:

Religion. Most cities in Egypt have a patron god that requires more attention than other deities in the city. In some cities, certain gods are completely unknown.

Floodplain Farms and Work Camps. Work Camps provide peasant labor (in the form of walkers) to floodplain farms. Floodplain farms do not directly employ their workers.

Gold. Gold can be mined from certain rock and converted into currency, measured in debens.

Tax Collection. Before you can collect taxes, a Palace must be functioning in the city. Tax collectors from the Tax Collector's offices will not be able to squeeze one deben from citizens unless the city has a Palace.

Luxury Goods. Foreign luxury goods, the commodities most prized by occupants of high-level housing, are very expensive to import. Due to the expense of safely transporting them across difficult terrain, it is not lucrative for a city to export luxury goods.

Now that you're familiar with the basic city-building tools, you're ready to begin building the most magnificent city Egypt has ever known.

Housing, Roads and Drinking Water

The first step to attracting people to your city is to designate areas for housing. When the first immigrants come to your city, they are content to live in rudimentary structures. As your city develops and its people become more sophisticated, they expect to build their homes into more impressive domiciles.

Your city needs roads if citizens are to move about. Only a few people, for example soldiers and immigrants, can leave the road. When you first arrive at your city site, you will notice a main road cutting through your land. Build more roads off this main road, line them with housing areas, and soon you will have neighborhoods teeming with activity.

Citizens also need your help in meeting their most basic need: water. Without drinking water, your citizens cannot survive for long.

These structures — housing, roads and water structures — are the most basic needs in any city. Mastering the art of constructing these structures gives you the fundamental knowledge you need to build a great city.

Your City Site

Before you begin building your city, take a look at the land on which you will establish it. Your city's site and the surrounding area has many different terrain types, each of which is suited for a different purpose.

Grassland. Grass grows on land near water, indicating that there is groundwater flowing underneath it. Because of this groundwater, you can place water-related structures on grassland.

Meadow. Meadows, identified by their yellow vegetation, can support farms (see page 62).

Flood plain. The flood plain is generally the most fertile land in Egypt. Found along the banks of the Nile, the land's fertility is restored each year when the Nile floods its banks (see page 59). Because of the annual flooding, farms, roads and Irrigation Ditches are the only structures that can be built on the flood plain.

Desert. Deserts are often a good place to build industries (see pages 68-79), but a poor place for housing because it is difficult to supply these areas with clean drinking water. Deserts cannot support water-related structures.

Sand Dunes. Sand dunes form when the desert wind blows. Nothing can be built on sand dunes, but people can walk over them.

Forest. If there is a forest in the area, you may be able to harvest wood (see page 72). You can also permanently cut down a forest by clearing the land (see page 38).

Marshland. Marshes are the habitat for reeds (see page 72), which can be made into papyrus. Marshland is found near water and sprouts very dark green reeds. Because the ground is so wet, you cannot build anything directly on the marsh, nor can you clear marshland.

Rock.   Rocky outcroppings sometimes indicate the presence of construction-grade stone, valuable ores or precious gemstones (see pages 69-71). Rock is impassable; people cannot walk over rock and must walk around it. You cannot build anything directly on rock.

Water.   The Nile carves a swath through many regions, and other areas may have oases or small ponds. Naturally, you cannot build any structures directly on the water.

The Kingdom Road

The Kingdom Road cuts through the city and links it to other cities in Egypt and the world. Immigrants also use the Kingdom road to get to your city. Be careful not to isolate your city from the Kingdom. Your city must have access to the rest of the Kingdom to survive.

Principles Guiding Construction

The same basic principles guide building most structures in the game. The rather large exceptions to the rule are monuments, which are discussed fully on pages 129-149. To build the rest of the buildings, the basic steps are:

1.   Clear the land, if necessary.
2.   Choose the appropriate button from the Control Panel.
3.   Place your building.

You will know if you are choosing an appropriate place for your building if you see a green "ghost" of it as you move the cursor over the desired location. If you see red, the land is not clear or the building you've chosen has special requirements which you have not yet met.

Clearing Land

Clear Land Button

With the exception of monuments, you must clear the land first before building a structure. To clear land, click on the "Clear Land" button on the Control Panel. When the special Dig cursor appears, click on the spot that you would like to clear. You can clear large areas at one time by dragging your cursor over the land. The land clears as you drag the mouse, and the amount of money needed to clear it is displayed. You can reshape the area of land you're clearing by repositioning the cursor, but once you let go of the mouse button, the land is cleared and the money is spent. If you change your mind, click the "Undo" button on the Control Panel. Do so quickly, however, because you have a limited amount of time in which to undo any action.

Undo Button

If a forest is blocking your way, think carefully before clearing it. Wood is an extremely rare and valuable commodity, and it may behoove you to change your city design instead of clearing the forest.

Building Roads

Most structures in *Pharaoh* need road access. If citizens

Egypt's Neighborhoods
Ahket, 12th year of Ramesses
Evening

Dear Journal

After the arduous task of unloading our ship's cargo, I was ready for a good night's sleep. I stationed a guard outside the Storage Yard we had procured for our goods and made my way to Khmunhotep's house. I met Khmunhotep last year, when he worked as a scribe who accompanied trade missions abroad. He told me that I would be most welcome in his house if ever I found myself in Egypt.

I made my way through the twisting and turning streets to Khmunhotep's neighborhood. It was clear to me as I walked that Egypt is much like other places I've been: not everyone shares equally in the land's wealth. Some of the homes were quite run down, while others were larger and kept up. I entered Khmunhotep's street where the homes were quite large. The residents were obviously well off, and most probably worked for the government.

Khmunhotep's home is filled with fine things that point to his status. His pottery is the finest available, and the clothing his family wears is made of very sheer linen, a mark of quality. He scents his home with myrrh, imported from Pwenet. Of course, these luxuries come with a price: he has one of the highest tax bills in the neighborhood.

Tired from my journey, I retired to bed. The typical Egyptian headrest, a curved piece of wood atop a small pedestal, didn't look especially inviting, but this wooden "pillow" proved to be surprisingly restful.

Road Button

can't get to a building via a road, they can't acquire the goods or services that building provides nor can they find employment there.

To build a road, first make sure the land is clear. Then, choose the "Road" button, and click on the area where you would like to place a road. Just as with clearing the land, you can build large sections of road at one time by clicking and dragging the mouse. As you drag

the mouse, you see what the road will look like after it's placed and how much it will cost. If there are any barriers, such as uncleared land or a building, the road bends around the obstruction. When you let go of the mouse button, the road is laid.

When neighborhoods begin to prosper, the city's residents take it upon themselves to pave over dirt roads. Once a road is paved, you can place Plazas on them (see pages 113-114).

Building Housing

Build Housing Button

You never build or improve housing directly. Rather, you define areas where you want people to settle, and they do the rest. When your city is new, some immigrants always show up to build homes as soon as you earmark the land for them. After this initial influx of people, your city must attract new citizens by offering the things people want — mainly food, jobs and housing.

To designate a housing area, first click on the "Housing" button on the Control Panel. Then, click on the area where you'd like to place some housing.

You can designate housing areas one lot at a time, or you can hold down the mouse button and drag over larger areas. You can even drag an area of housing over roads — the roads remain in place. After you earmark an area for housing, a "vacant" sign appears on the land. When immigrants arrive, they will construct their own simple structures.

All housing must be placed within two spaces of the road and must be built on clear land. Make sure there is a clear path between the housing areas you designate and the Kingdom Road. You may need to build water crossings (see pages 110-113) so that immigrants can get to certain areas.

Housing Evolution

As conditions improve in the city, your citizens will want to live in more attractive structures. They will upgrade their housing on their own. The advantages of highly evolved housing are many, including increased tax revenues and improved prosperity (see page 192). All you need to do to foster the development of better housing is to make sure your citizens live in pleasant neighborhoods and have access to the goods and services they want.

Dilapidated houses drag down the desirability of the surrounding area. Ramshackle housing catches fire easily; as housing improves, the chance that it will catch on fire decreases. Fine homes also enhance the desirability of the surrounding area, perhaps even helping other nearby houses to evolve into better domiciles.

Goods and Services

What do your citizens want? Their needs aren't much different from our own. They like a varied diet and goods, such as pottery, linen and beer, that make their lives easier and more fun. As your citizens become wealthier, they also want luxury goods, both domestic and imported, in their homes. The chapters on food and farming (pages 59-67) and industry (pages 69-79) will tell you how to provide these items.

Access to services, such as education (pages 165-166), religion (pages 117-127) and entertainment (pages 159-163), enriches your people's lives and encourages them to build more impressive homes.

Desirability

Citizens will improve their housing if you surround

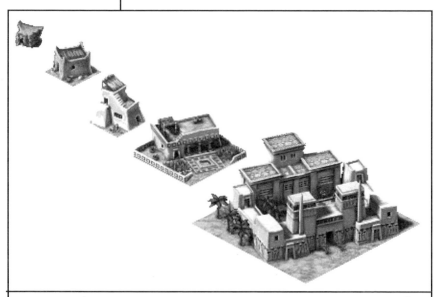

Housing Evolution. As conditions in your city improve, your citizens will take it upon themselves to build more elaborate dwellings.

them with beauty. Neighborhoods with lush Gardens and stately Statues are most appreciated by your citizens.

Equally important to adding attractive elements is keeping unattractive elements to a minimum. Your citizens won't relish living near noisy and smelly industrial structures or buildings that unsavory characters frequent. For more on each building's particular effect on desirability, consult Appendix 1, starting on page 222.

The easiest way to find out what a specific dwelling needs to evolve, or what is preventing it from evolving, is to info-click on it. The pop-up screen tells you exactly what the house needs next to evolve. It also provides an inventory of household goods. This inventory shows you if the dwelling is about to run out of anything which might hinder its future development.

Wells and Water Supplies

Wells and Water Supplies provide drinking water to your populace. These structures cannot be placed just anywhere — they must be built on grassland (see page 36). Grassland indicates the presence of groundwater. A green "ghost" of the water structure will appear when you have chosen a viable location. You can also use the Water Overlay (see page 204) to see which land can support water-related structures.

Health and Sanitation
Structures Button

A Well is the most basic water structure. It provides access to fairly clean drinking water to a limited range of homes. While some water is better than no water, a Well is less beneficial than its cousin, the Water Supply.

Well

Water Supply

Water Supplies need road access and employees to carry the water to nearby homes. Water Supplies and their water carriers can cover a wider area of your city than Wells can, and the water they provide is much cleaner than that provided by Wells.

Water Supplies also help reduce the risk of malaria striking the city (see page 154).

People and Employment

As the city grows, it comes alive with people going about their daily tasks. New families arrive, others depart. The workforce tends to its responsibilities, bringing services to the citizens. Men, women and children are all active participants in city life. They are the city's lifeblood, coursing along its streets. The citizens' lives — how they come to your city, how they find employment, and what happens after they attain wealth — are the topics of this chapter.

Attracting Immigrants

When the city is new, immigrants in search of adventure come to experience life on a new frontier. As the city becomes more established, new immigrants are attracted mainly as a result of word-of-mouth. If life in the city is good, resulting in high City Sentiment, then the residents will spread the word throughout the Kingdom. New people will come to the city provided there is room for them.

City Sentiment

City Sentiment is an indicator of the quality of life in the city. The factors that contribute to high City Sentiment are high wages, low taxes, food availability and job availability. All citizens expect to be properly fed and to be employed. They also expect to be adequately compensated for their work and not to pay an unreasonable tax rate.

Citizens are well aware of what wages other Egyptian cities pay. If the Kingdom's standard wage level changes, a message notifying you of the new pay rate will be sent.

You can get away with charging citizens higher taxes if the city is otherwise a great place to live. Citizens won't mind paying a little extra to live in a city with plenty of food, jobs and decent wages. Citizens will become upset, however, if they feel conditions are

---

Khmunhotep's Family
Ahket, 12th year of Ramesses
Morning
Dear Journal,

Nefernetka, Khmunhotep's wife, greeted me when I finally arose in the morning. She offered me a delicious porridge of grain for breakfast. While I was eating, the children came in to see the newcomer. All the children still have the 'side lock of youth': their hair is cut short except for a long tress of hair that comes from the side of their heads. The eldest, who is nearly 14, will soon have this side lock cut off and endure the sebi ceremony in which he will be circumcised. Once he has entered adulthood, his family will send him to the Per-Ankh, which we call library, to learn his father's craft.

After the children returned to their toys, Nefernetka told me of a recent misfortune that befell her family. Her father passed on after a long and fruitful life. Nefernetka misses her father terribly, but takes comfort in the knowledge that he lives on in the Field of Reeds. Nefernetka also rests easy knowing that, in accordance with Egyptian tradition, one-third of her father's estate passes to Nefernetka's mother. Nefernetka and her siblings share the other two-thirds. At least the family is free from want.

After breakfast, I left Khmunhotep's home to negotiate a trade on behalf of my country.

unfair in the city. If half the citizens are paying high taxes, and the other half are paying no taxes at all, City Sentiment will plummet.

If you fail to meet citizens' expectations, the word will quickly spread to others considering a move to your city. Potential immigrants will decide to stay where they are or find another city to call home if your city has a poor reputation, as expressed by the low sentiment of its residents. If your city's reputation drops too precipitously, some of its residents may move out in search of a better life.

Your Chief Overseer (see page 203) knows how citizens are feeling. Use his City Sentiment report as a guide to improving conditions in your city.

In addition to limiting immigration, poor City Sentiment can also encourage crime (see page 99).

Lack of housing is the other major factor that keeps immigrants away. Check in with your Overseer of the Granaries (see page 200). He can tell you how many more people the city's current housing stock can host. If housing is almost completely occupied, zone some new housing areas to attract new immigrants, or take steps to encourage existing homes to improve. Better housing accommodates more people.

Finding Workers

Most buildings require employees (you'll learn about the different jobs your citizens can have in subsequent chapters). When a new building needing employees is built, it dispatches a representative to seek out available workers in nearby neighborhoods. If he finds occupied housing nearby, and if the city overall has people in need of work, then the building that sent him out will be staffed with employees. If he fails to find a staff for the building that sent him, he'll continue his search.

People of the City

The city employs dozens of different workers who perform very different tasks. Some of the city's workers make their way along the city's streets as they go about their day-to-day tasks. These walkers can be broken down into two groups: those that have a specific destination in mind and those who roam the city.

Destination Walkers

Destination walkers leave their places of employment with a specific goal in mind. Using a map of your city's roads, they determine the shortest route to their destination. With few exceptions (noted below), they always use your city's roads to find the shortest route.

Your city's destination walkers are:

> Buyers from the Bazaar
> Delivery men (cart pushers, sled pullers and
>   chariot deliverers)
> Thieves
> Vagrants
> Tower and wall sentries
> Sledge haulers (do not need roads)
> Hunters (do not need roads)
> Reed gatherers (do not need roads)
> Wood cutters (do not need roads)
> Soldiers (do not need roads)
> Immigrants (do not need roads)
> Emigrants (do not need roads)

These people always make a trip for a specific purpose, usually to pick up or deliver something.

Certain people who normally roam freely will sometimes have a specific destination in mind:

> Performers on their way from performer's schools to venues
> Constables on their way to defend the city
> Fire marshals on their way to douse a fire
> Stonemasons, bricklayers and carpenters on their way to a monument

Unless the above walkers are performing the tasks specified, they behave as roaming walkers.

Roaming Walkers

Walkers who roam the city bring benefits to your citizens when they pass by housing. Some also provide valuable services to the buildings in the city.

Roamers leave their buildings with no specific destination in mind. When they leave their building, they try to start in a different direction every time. From there, they can be completely unpredictable.

Every time walkers who roam the city encounter an intersection, they must decide which way to turn. They don't make the same decision every time, so houses that they have passed before may not be visited again for some time.

The best way to corral these walkers is through good city planning. Since intersections give these walkers so much freedom, keeping intersections to a minimum helps to guide these walkers to where you want them to go.

Roadblocks (see page 109) are another effective tool in controlling roamers. When a roamer encounters a Roadblock, he or she turns around. Walkers with a specific destination in mind pass through Roadblocks.

Use Roadblocks carefully. If you place a Roadblock to prevent a Bazaar seller from strolling through the city's industrial sector, for example, you might also block architects and fire marshals who need to service some industrial buildings on the other side of the Roadblock. Roadblocks that separate industries from housing can also prevent buildings from finding needed employees. Roadblocks can make no distinction between roamers, so carefully consider who you might be blocking out when you use them.

The walkers who roam the city are:

> Bazaar sellers
> Constables (except as noted on page 51)
> Magistrates
> Fire marshals (except as noted on page 51)
> Architects
> Performers (except as noted on page 51)
> Bricklayers (except as noted on page 51)
> Carpenters (except as noted on page 51)
> Stonemasons (except as noted on page 51)
> Senet masters
> Priests

Teachers
Librarians
Plagued citizens
Tax collectors
Dentists
Physicians
Herbalists
Embalmers
Water carriers

If your city's housing has evolved to very high levels (see page 41), you may also see scribes wandering around your city. Scribes enjoy the city's services, but do not work themselves. For more on scribes, see page 57.

Unemployment

Unemployment can become a serious problem in your city, but one that is relatively easy to solve. High unemployment contributes to poor City Sentiment (see page 47) which can hamper immigration and encourage crime.

The cure to unemployment is to create new jobs. Unemployment affords you the opportunity to improve your city's services, which could lead to a higher Culture Rating (see page 191). Check in with your Overseers (see pages 197-203) to see if your city has an adequate number of entertainment venues, Temples, Schools, Libraries and health facilities. If the city is lacking in any of these areas, solve the unemployment problem by building more structures to provide the needed services. Use the Overlays (see pages 203-209) to see if any specific neighborhoods in the city lack particular services.

You can also turn unemployment problems into cold, hard debens. If the city is engaging in trade, check to see it is exporting all that it can to its trade partners. If it isn't, build more of the required industry to meet the demand. The city's coffers will benefit.

A low level of unemployment is actually better than a labor shortage. New buildings draw their workers from the ranks of the unemployed. When more than 10 percent of citizens are out of work, though, problems will ensue.

Labor Shortages

Labor shortages can be the more devastating employment problem. When industries are understaffed, services begin to suffer because buildings that are only partially staffed are much less efficient than fully staffed buildings. When services suffer, property values go down and people are usually forced from their homes, sometimes causing emigration. Emigration, of course, further reduces the workforce which results in more services suffering.

Drawing immigrants to the city solves labor shortage problems. If the city is currently experiencing a labor shortage, manage the labor force (see below) to make sure that key services, like food production and distribution, are fully staffed.

Managing Labor

Your Overseer of the Workers (page 197) and your Overseer of Commerce (page 199) can help you manage the city's labor force to alleviate a labor shortage.

To ensure that the most important services are provided, work with your Overseer of the Workers to set employment priorities. The Overseer lists all the employment sectors in the city, the number of workers required in each sector, and the current number of workers employed in each sector. If one of the sectors that you consider to be most important is understaffed, click on it. A screen pops up with the numbers one through nine. Click the number one to make the selected sector the top priority. The Overseer of the Workers funnels employees into the work sector you've designated the top priority until all positions in that sector are filled. After you set a first priority, you

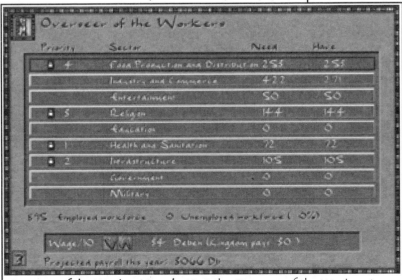

Overseer of the Workers' Panel. Visit the Overseer of the Workers to set labor allocation priorities. The Overseer will fill the prioritized job sectors first.

can set a second, then a third, and so on.

You can prioritize the labor force in any order you wish. You can only have one top priority, though, and when you choose a new one, your other priorities are adjusted accordingly. Note that when you set priorities, other employment sectors can suffer from severe labor shortages.

Your Overseer of Commerce can also help solve a labor shortage by shutting down industries. Check the city's Storage Yards and Granaries for good candidates for temporary work stoppage. If you notice that the city has a glut of a particular supply, shut that industry down for a while. That industry's employees will find work in other employment sectors and help to reduce the labor shortage.

To temporarily shut down an industry, visit the Overseer of Commerce and click on the industry you wish to shut down. On the screen that pops up, a button reading "Industry is On" appears. Click the button until it reads "Industry is Off" to shut it down. To turn an industry back on, click the button until it reads "Industry is On." When in industry has been shut down, it will appear in yellow on the Overseer of Commerce's screen.

Keep an eye on the Storage Yards while industries are shut down to make sure the city doesn't run out of any goods it needs. Also be careful when shutting down a raw material producer. If the city runs out of a raw material, manufacturers that require the item won't be able to turn out any new goods, and their employees will sit idle unless you specifically shut down their industry, too.

Scribes

When your city matures into a fine metropolis that offers the best of goods, services and, most important-ly, education, some citizens become scribes. Scribes do not work, but they do pay a lot in taxes. You can watch them going about your city, pursuing leisure.

When some of your working folk become scribes, the demand for goods may increase, but your pool of available workers *decreases*. If immigrants don't pour into your city to take the newly vacant positions, take steps to lure more immigrants.

Farming and Food Production

Zoning land for houses gets people to the city. Food keeps them there. Food production is probably the single most important industry in the city, and farms will likely be the primary source of food. The city won't survive long without a steady source of food. Hungry people tend to be cranky, prone to disease and eager emigrants.

Most of Egypt is dry and unarable. The fertile banks of the Nile, however, cut through like a rich, luxurious ribbon. This fertile land is limited, so you must plan farms carefully. Other areas have meadows on which farms can thrive.

The Nile, the Inundation and the Nilometer

Certainly, many great cities and countries have been built along the banks of a river. What makes the Nile so special? Each year, the Nile floods its banks, depositing nutrient-rich silt on the land. Called the Inundation, this yearly event is so important that Egyptians base their seasons on the river's cycles.

Usually, the Nile floods its banks every year between June and September. Two to four months after the flood, the Nile recedes, leaving behind it the most fertile land in Egypt.

But, the Nile is unpredictable. It can flood high one year and low the next, or, if your city is truly unfortunate, the flood might not happen at all. Luckily, you have a Nilometer to help you gauge the coming flood's characteristics. Priests interpret the Nilometer readings and notify your Chief Overseer (page 203) with information regarding the next flood. Check in with your Chief Overseer for the latest Nilometer reading so you can plan for the coming year and adjust food production as necessary.

The only things you can build on the flood plain are farms, roads and Irrigation Ditches. All other buildings would be destroyed by the flood.

Building Food and Farming Structures

Food and Farming
Structures Button

All the structures in this section can be built by clicking on the "Food and Farming Structures" button in the Control Panel. The menu that pops up lists all the food and farming structures available to you. Some regions may not be able to support all types of farms and food structures.

Floodplain Farming and Work Camps

Farming on the flood plain can be very productive. Acre for acre, floodplain farms tend to yield more crops than meadow farms (see page 62), but the growing season is limited due to the Inundation, and the farms are harvested only once every year.

Floodplain farms generally produce more because the land there is usually more fertile. Not all floodplain land, however, is equally fertile. The darker the flood plain and the lusher the grass growing on it, the more fertile it is. Info-click on a farm to find out its land's fertility.

The flood plain's fertility depends upon the flood's waters. Every time a farm on the flood plain is harvested, the fertility of the land is depleted. If the flood waters do not replenish the land, its fertility is not restored. If the floodplain land you have built farms on begins to lose its fertility, you might consider building new farms on more fertile land and demolishing the old ones.

Peasant Life
Ahket, 12th year of Ramesses
Midday
Dear Journal,

　　As I walked towards the Storage Yard where our items for trade were stored, I thought how fortuitous our timing was. The Inundation was due to start in a couple of weeks, and all the crops had just been harvested. Egypt's Granaries are filled to capacity right now, and I'm sure the trade minister will be eager to unload some of the surplus.

　　The Nile is truly a blessing to this land. Without it, Egypt would be like so many lands in this region: hot, dry and infertile. Because the river fertilizes the land each year, Egypt is able to grow diverse crops like grain, barley, flax, chickpeas, pomegranates and figs, to name but a few. The Inundation is remarkably reliable, too. Granted, some years the Inundation is lower than in others, but only on the rarest occasion has the Inundation been too low to fertilize the land.

　　As I walked through the peasants' neighborhood, I saw the men of the households preparing for their journeys to the desert where they will help build Pharaoh's tomb. The government conscripted many of these men to do this hard work, but the workers will be paid. Most of them consider it an honor to help Pharaoh to immortality.

Floodplain farms also tend to produce more because they do not need to devote space for year-round living quarters. Floodplain farms are just fields, and any required farm hands come from a Work Camp.

Work Camp

Gangs of peasants gather at the Work Camp for assignment. During farming season, the Work Camp will likely send most of its work crews to the floodplain farms. If all floodplain farms are staffed, or if it is flood season, the Work Camp sends gangs to work on any active monument projects in the city that may need them.

While one Work Camp could provide peasants for all floodplain farms and monuments, the more Work Camps you have, the quicker farms or construction projects will receive the peasants they need. More Work Camps will also provide more peasants, which speeds the monument-building process.

Like other walkers, peasant laborers have a limited working life. Time spent walking to work is time not spent working, so don't build Work Camps too far from the floodplain fields.

Both Work Camps and floodplain farms require road access. Work Camps also need labor.

Meadow Farming

Arable land is not limited to the flood plains. Meadows are also arable, and meadow farms have the advantage of supporting crops year-round.

Meadow Farm

Work Camps do not supply meadow farms with a gang of farm hands; rather, each meadow farm must find its own staff of employees. Fully staffing the farm is important; a farm that is partially staffed yields less than a fully-staffed farm. In addition to labor, meadow farms need road access.

When building a farm, you don't have to specify "Meadow Farm" or "Floodplain Farm." Your architects automatically know which type of farm to build, depending on where you build it. Both farms cost the same amount of money.

Depending on the crop, meadow farms are harvested one or two times per year. Barley, grain and pomegranates are harvested twice a year, while flax, lettuce and chickpeas are harvested only once a year. Each harvest usually produces less than a floodplain farm's harvest.

Fertility varies from meadow to meadow. The yellow vegetation that grows on meadows with high fertility is very dense. Harvesting a meadow farm does not deplete the fertility of its land. Info-clicking on a meadow farm shows you the fertility level of its land and when the next harvest will be.

Meadow farms can be vital to the city's existence. While harvests of floodplain farms are large, they only occur once a year, and the farms are inactive for two to four months of the year during the Inundation. Because they are active year round, meadow farms can help tide the population over during the Inundation.

Irrigation and Water Lifts

You can increase the fertility — and hence, the pro-

Water Lift

ductivity — of farmland through irrigation. Irrigation can turn land that yields little into land that can support a productive farm. Both floodplain and meadow farmland can be irrigated.

To bring the benefits of irrigation to a farm, run an Irrigation Ditch to within two spaces of it. The effects of irrigation are not cumulative; as long as there is one Irrigation Ditch within two spaces of a farm, the farm is fully irrigated.

Floodplain farms are at the water's level where Irrigation Ditches can be connected directly to the Nile. Meadow farms, however, are not at the water's level. To irrigate meadow farms, you must build a Water Lift.

Water Lifts bring water up one level. They can be built on land adjacent to a body of water or to the flood plain. For Water Lifts built adjacent to the flood plain, you must build an Irrigation Ditch running from the Nile to the front of the Water Lift to supply it with water.

Attach an Irrigation Ditch to the back of the Water Lift to irrigate meadow farms. Irrigation Ditches twist and turn around all objects that impede their path except for roads. Irrigation Ditches automatically run under roads as needed.

Increasing the fertility of its land will increase the amount of food a farm yields.

Fertility has no effect on the length of the growing season.

Even irrigated farms must still be built on arable land. Irrigation can increase the fertility of land, but it cannot make infertile land fertile.

Crop Types

Egypt can grow many types of crops. Most locations, however, can only support a few different types, and some desert areas can grow nothing at all and must import all their food. Some farms grow foodstuffs that will keep citizens fed while other farms grow crops which are used for raw materials.

The foods grown on farms are grain, chickpeas, lettuce, pomegranates and figs. Grain Farms also produce straw as a by-product, which is used in the manufacture of bricks (see page 76) and also to feed cattle (see page 67). The other raw materials produced on farms are barley and flax. Barley Farms grow barley that is brewed into beer (see page 76), and Flax Farms produce flax that is woven into linen (see page 76).

Other Food Sources

Egypt's bounty isn't limited to what can be produced on farms. Many regions have an abundance of wildlife that can be hunted. The Nile's waters, essential to the success of farms, also teem with fish. And, cattle can be raised for the meat they provide. Here's what you'll need to do to take advantage of these resources:

Hunting. Animals that can be hunted live in herds or flocks. If you notice a herd or flock of one of the types of animals listed below, build a

Hunting Lodge

Hunting Lodge nearby. Hunting Lodges train and equip hunters to skillfully kill their quarry. Animals that can be hunted for food are:

> Ostriches
> Water Fowl
> Antelope

Hunters will never completely wipe out all the animals, but herd and flock size nevertheless is limited, as is the rate at which they are replenished. Game meat from hunting is a good supplement to citizens' diets or a good way to feed a small population. Herds obviously do not grow larger as the city's population increases; therefore, game meat will make up a smaller percentage of the city's food stock as the city grows.

Fishing. Not all waterways support fish. If a body of water has fish, you will see them periodically leaping out of the water into the air. To use these fish for food, the city needs one or more fishing boats.

Fishing Wharf

Fishing boats are berthed at Fishing Wharves. Shipwrights (see page 77) build boats for the industries in the city that need them. Fishing Wharves and Shipwrights must be built on straight sections of coast, and half of the structure must overhang the water so that vessels can have access to them. If the city has a working Shipwright, building a Fishing Wharf signals the ship builders to get busy building a fishing boat.

Like herds, fish stocks are limited but cannot be completely depleted. A large population will flounder if it tries to subsist solely on fish.

Raising Cattle. Cattle Ranches can be built anywhere, even in desert areas. Cattle eat straw that
can either be grown on Grain Farms or imported
from a trade partner.

Cattle Ranch

Cattle Ranches store this straw on site to keep the
cattle fed.

Hunting Lodges, Fishing Wharves and Cattle Ranches
all require road access and workers.

Industry

People have built attractive housing, and immigrants are pouring in. You have working farms to feed the populace and to provide some employment. Now, your people are demanding more. They want more goods and services, and more jobs for themselves. To provide for these needs, a city must have a bustling economy supported by industry.

Types of Industries

A multitude of industries flourish in Egypt, and your city will most likely be able to support many of them. Some industries produce raw materials, other industries turn those raw materials into finished products. All industries have two very basic requirements: access to the road and a labor supply.

Industrial Structures
Button

Raw Materials

Egypt is blessed with many resources that can be manufactured into goods. These resources, however, must be coaxed from the earth; they do not just present themselves at manufacturers, ready to be used. To harvest raw materials, click on Industrial Structures: Raw Materials, then choose a structure. You'll find these raw materials in Egypt:

Stone. Quarrymen chisel large blocks of rock at four different kinds of quarry:

Plain stone Quarry
Limestone Quarry
Granite Quarry
Sandstone Quarry

Quarry

If there are extensive rocky outcroppings in the city's area, you are most likely able to build quarries to extract the rock. Some areas, though, will have rock that's not of construction grade, or too little rock to support industry. Click on the Industrial Structures button and check the list of raw materials available. This list shows you what types of stone, if any, can be quarried in the area.

You must build quarries adjacent to rocky outcroppings. If you have picked an appropriate location, you will see a green ghost of the Quarry you're trying to place. Otherwise, you will see a red block.

Stone cannot be manufactured into other products. Stone is, however, the stuff of monuments, and significant amounts of stone are needed to complete even some of the smaller monuments.

Quarries, which are dug into the side of rocky outcroppings, are prone to collapse. Be sure to build an Architect's post (see page 100) near the quarries to prevent disaster.

Gold and Copper. Metallic nuggets lying amongst rocky outcroppings indicate the presence of gold, copper or both. Click on the Industrial Structures button and check the raw materials list to see which, if any, you can mine.

Metal Mine

If you are lucky enough to be able to mine gold, you should take advantage of the opportunity. Gold is money, and mining gold affords your city the chance to make its own.

Before you start mining gold, build a Palace (see page 101). The Palace converts gold ore into usable currency, which is counted in debens. If gold is mined before a Palace is built, the Gold Mine's cart pusher will have no place to take it. Gold ore is never stored in a Storage Yard.

Copper is a valuable metal, too. After it has been mined, copper can be sold to trade partners or manufactured into weapons at a Weaponsmith (see page 77).

Both Copper and Gold Mines must be built next to rocky outcroppings with metallic nuggets. When trying to place a mine, a green ghost of the building will appear when you hold your mouse cursor over a viable location.

Copper and Gold Mines, like Quarries, are in danger of collapsing. Build an Architect's post nearby to help deter this risk.

Gems. Gems, like stone, gold and copper, are mined from rocky outcroppings. You can't tell by looking at the rock whether or not it can produce gems. If gems can be mined, Gemstone Mines will be listed in the Industrial Structures: Raw Materials list. Like quarries, Gemstone Mines must be placed adjacent to rocky outcroppings. They are also susceptible to collapse, so be sure to build an Architect's post nearby.

Gemstone Mine

Farm

Straw, Barley and Flax. Barley, flax and straw are grown on farms. Raw material farms like these share all the characteristics common to food farms: they must be built on arable land, their fields become more fertile with irrigation and farms built on the flood plain tend to yield more crops. See the chapter on Food and Farming on pages 58-67 for more information.

Barley Farms produce barley from which Brewers make beer (page 76), and flax that can be made into linen (page 76) grows on Flax Farms. Straw grows on Grain Farms (page 65) and is a by-product of grain production. Straw, along with clay, is used to make bricks (page 76), and straw is also used to feed cattle on Cattle Ranches (page 67).

Reeds and Wood. If you see stands of trees or fields of reeds, you can usually build a Reed Gatherer or a Wood Cutter. Just as the presence of small stone deposits doesn't always mean that you can quarry stone, some areas of trees or reeds might be too small, or of too low quality, to support industry. You'll know for sure if you have access to these buildings if they are in the Industrial Structures: Raw Materials list.

Reed Gatherer

A Reed Gatherer sends out harvesters to collect reeds that can be pounded into papyrus at the Papyrus Maker. A Reed Gatherer does not have to be adjacent to a field of reeds. Harvesters are willing to walk from their building to the reed field.

Wood Cutter

A Wood Cutter works in a similar fashion. Like

the Reed Gatherer, the Wood Cutter does not have to be adjacent to a forest.

Wood is an important and valuable raw material in Egypt and the rest of the world. Shipwrights (see page 77) need wood to construct and repair warships and transport ships. Chariot Makers construct chariots from wood (see page 77). Finally, wood is used by the Carpenters' Guild to make ramps and scaffolding for monuments (see page 130).

Wood tends to be scarce in Egypt, so you should harvest it whenever you have the chance. Because it is so rare, think twice before clearing trees in order to make room for buildings. Wood is one of the more valuable raw materials in the open market, and your city can profit from exporting it.

While neither the Reed Gatherer nor the Wood Cutter needs to be built next to their raw material, it makes sense to place these buildings as close to the raw material as possible. The shorter the distance the workers have to travel, the more productive they will be.

When harvesters and wood cutters are about their tasks, you'll notice that after they have harvested a region, the reeds or trees do not grow back right away. It takes time for new reeds and trees to sprout and grow. Because of this, it is possible to over-harvest these resources if you have too many harvesters or wood cutters working in a particular area. Reeds and trees (unless you clear them) will eventually grow back, but your industries might sit idle while waiting for regrowth. It's best to consider the amount of resources available before building Wood Cutters and Reed Gatherers.

Clay Pit. Clay Pits produce clay that can be turned into pottery by a Potter (see page 75). When combined with straw, clay can also be turned into brick (see page 76), an important construction material for certain monuments.

Clay Pit

Clay Pits need to be near a body of water because that is where the best quality clay is found. You'll know that you've picked a good spot for a Clay Pit when you see a green ghost of the building.

All raw materials producers employ delivery men, either cart pushers or sled pullers, that bring their

materials to other buildings that need them. The delivery men first try to find a manufacturer that needs supplies. Because they don't like to work any harder than necessary, they always try to bring their raw materials to the closest manufacturer. If no manufacturer needs their load of raw materials, the delivery men find the closest Storage Yard that has space for their load.

The only raw material delivery men who do not behave in this fashion are the Gold Mine cart pusher and the quarry sled puller. The Gold Mine cart pusher brings his gold only to the Palace, never to a Storage Yard. Because stone cannot be manufactured into any other good, quarry sled pullers always bring their materials to a Storage Yard.

Each raw material producer generally furnishes enough commodity to supply two manufacturers.

Manufacturers

To really rake in the trade debens, build manufacturers to turn raw materials into finished goods. Manufactured goods tend to have a higher market value than raw materials. Furthermore, citizens have little use for raw materials directly, though they clamor for manufactured goods.

All manufacturers function similarly. They all require road access and labor. They all also require raw materials delivered to them from a raw material producer or a Storage Yard. If the city cannot produce a raw material that manufacturers need, the city will be able to import it from a trade partner.

To build most manufacturers, choose the Industrial Structures button from the Control Panel, then pick a manufacturer. The only manufacturers that are not listed here are the Weaponsmith and the Chariot Maker. These structures can be built by clicking on the Military Structures button on the Control Panel.

Following is a complete list of all manufactured products. Because access to different raw materials is limited, not all regions will be able to manufacture all the products listed.

> **Pottery.** Potters turn clay into pottery. Pottery is an important commodity in any city. It's the first good your citizens will demand after you satisfy their needs for food and water.

Potter

Brewery

Weaver

Jeweler

Papyrus Maker

Brickworks

Beer. Brewers take the humble barley plant and transform it into tasty beer at the Brewery. Like pottery, beer is one of the products your citizens want to have in their homes. Beer is also served at the Senet House (see page 161).

Linen. Weavers turn flax fibers into linen. Your citizens use linen for clothing and want a supply of the material in their homes. Mortuaries (see page 152) also use linen to perform the embalming ritual.

Luxury Goods. Your richest citizens want fine luxury goods, and they won't be satisfied with just one type. The only luxury good you'll be able to manufacture, however, is jewelry from gemstones. Jewelers craft these fine pieces in their workshops. To meet your wealthy citizens' demands, your city will need to import a second luxury good from a trade partner at significant cost.

While jewelry is expensive to import, it is not a lucrative export for your city. Much of the expense in buying a luxury good is the cost of transportation, not the cost of materials.

Papyrus. Papyrus Makers hammer reeds into papyrus. Papyrus is essential to education (see page 165) in your city. You must have a supply of papyrus stored in your Storage Yard to build a Library, and both Libraries and Scribal Schools need papyrus to educate your wealthiest citizens.

Bricks. Brick makers combine clay with straw to make bricks. Bricks are essential to the construction of certain monuments (see pages 132-134,

141-142).

Weapons. Using copper, the Weaponsmith fashions weapons. The Recruiter uses weapons to equip Infantry companies (see page 171).

Weaponsmith

Chariots. The Chariot Maker uses wood to manufacture magnificent war chariots. He sends the finished product to the Recruiter to outfit charioteers (see page 171).

Chariot Maker

Ships. Shipwrights build and repair all ships in your city (except for ferry boats). They are skilled in all types of boat making and can build a strong combat vessel just as easily as they can build a small fishing boat.

Shipwright

Shipwrights make fishing boats from whatever resources they have on hand and do not need a delivery of raw materials to fashion them. Warships and transport ships, on the other hand, are built from wood. Shipwrights need a supply of wood before they can begin building military ships.

Shipwrights need road access and workers. They also need to be placed on the coastline. You'll know when you've chosen a good spot when you see a green ghost of the building.

No water vessels are available for import or export.

Storage

Finished goods and excess raw materials are stored in Storage Yards (see page 84-85). These items can be exported from the city's Storage Yards, and Storage Yard delivery men bring finished goods and raw materials to buildings that require them. Storage Yards and their role within the city are discussed fully in the next chapter.

Running Efficient Industries

Efficient industries are profitable industries. The more goods an industry turns out, the more money can be made on the open market, or the better supplied your citizens will be with the products and services they crave. Providing plenty of workers for the city's industries is a good way to keep them active. An understaffed industry will turn out products at a much slower rate.

When you plan your city's industries, make sure raw materials producers are near their corresponding manufacturers. The longer a raw materials delivery man has to travel to make his delivery, the more likely it is that a manufacturer may fall idle in the meantime.

Commerce and Trade

Your farms produce succulent foods. Your industries turn out fine products and useful raw materials. How do you get the food and products your citizens demand to them? And how do you engage trade partners? The key is to fully develop your city's distribution system. An efficiently organized storage and distribution system will help you meet your citizens demands for commodities, increase the productivity of your industries and boost your city's profits from trade.

Granaries

Once farmers harvest their crops, hunters prepare their quarry, fishermen clean their catch and cattle ranchers carve their meat, the food needs someplace to go. That someplace is the Granary.

Granary

Each food farm and food-producing structure employs a cart pusher. These burly fellows are responsible for safely delivering food to the Granary. They will always seek out the closest Granary first, but will travel a great distance if all the nearby Granaries have no room for their product. If all the Granaries in the city have no room, or if they are understaffed and are not working properly, cart pushers stand still, confounded, until a Granary can accept his food again. Info-click on a stagnant cart pusher to find out why he isn't moving.

Cart pushers will bring their loads to a Storage Yard (see page 84-85), again favoring the closest one, if you have specifically told the Storage Yard to Accept a particular food. The cart pusher, in fact, will bypass the

Granary and take food directly to a Storage Yard if you set the Storage Yard's special orders (see page 85) for a particular food to Accept. From the Storage Yards, the food can be exported to a trade partner.

You can see at a glance how full a Granary is by looking through its fill holes at the foodstuffs stored inside. Info-click on the Granary to see exactly how much food and which types are stored there.

To build a Granary, click on the Storage and Distribution Structures button on the Control Panel. Granaries need both road access and labor.

Granary Special Orders

As your city grows, you might want to give specific orders to certain Granaries to manage the flow of food in your city. You can give Granaries instructions by choosing Special Orders from the panel that appears when you info-click on a Granary.

In the Special Orders panel, all the types of food available to your city are listed. The default setting is for the Granary to "Accept All" foods to the maximum amount the Granary can hold. By clicking the button next to the foodstuff, you can choose one of the following commands for each item:

Accept All/Fill Granary. You may decide to limit how much of a single item a Granary accepts (for example, to ensure the Granary carries a variety of Foods). You can tell the Granary to Fill anywhere from 1/4 to 3/4 of the Granary, or not to limit the amount and Accept All of the foodstuff. Use the scroll buttons at the far right of each item to set a limit on how much the Granary will accept.

Don't Accept.   If you want a Granary to stop accepting a type of food altogether, click on the button until "Don't Accept" appears. The Granary will not accept any more deliveries of that particular food, but Bazaar buyers and other Granaries can continue to collect the food until the supply is completely depleted.

Get Up To. If a Granary runs low on a food you would like to have on hand, tell it to go get the particular food. You can specify how much of an item you would like by using the scroll buttons to the right of the food. The Granary's cart pushers will go to other Granaries or to Storage Yards searching for the food, and will continue to go after a particular item until they have met the Granary's quota. Cart pushers will not collect food from Granaries that have the same "Get" order. Otherwise, the Granaries' cart pushers would spend their time swapping the same load of that commodity back and forth.

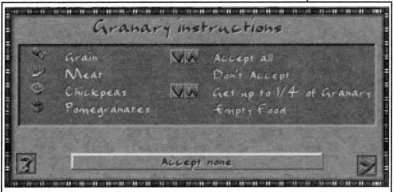

Granary Orders. Give the Granary special orders to manipulate the flow of food.

Empty Food. If you want a Granary to stop carrying a particular food, click on the button until "Empty Food" appears. The Granary's cart pushers will work to find another place for the food stuff until the Granary's stock of that particular item is depleted.

Storage Yards

Once the city's manufacturers have turned out their products, they need a place to send them to be stored. Storage Yards are the repository for all finished goods and also provide a place for excess raw materials or food. Storage Yards are also key to trade.

To build a Storage Yard, click on the Storage and Distribution Structures button on the Control Panel. You will see Storage Yard in the list that pops up. To function properly, Storage Yards need road access and labor.

Once the Storage Yard is operational, delivery men from the city's industries and food producers (if the Storage Yard's special orders are set to Accept food) make their way to the Storage Yard to deposit their loads. You can see the items stacked in the yard.

Each Storage Yard is divided into eight sections and can hold up to eight different items. Each section can hold only one type of item, but more than one section can store the same item. The quantity of each item that can be stored depends upon the item's size. The larger the item, the less of it a Storage Yard can store. For example, a Storage Yard can hold many more pieces of pottery than it can blocks of stone. To ensure efficient use of Storage Yard space, consider using Special Orders (see below).

To find out exactly how much of each item is stored in the Storage Yard, info-click on it. The screen that pops up lists how much of each item the particular Storage Yard has on hand and whether or not it can accept more goods. If a Storage Yard can't hold anymore of a particular item, the item is displayed in yellow.

Storage Yards employ cart pushers to deliver raw materials to manufacturers that need them and to pick up goods if they have been given special orders to do so.

Special Orders

You can give Storage Yards special orders to manage the flow of goods through the city. These orders are identical to the ones for the Granaries (described above on page 82):

> accept all/fill
> don't accept
> get
> empty

Use these orders to decide which items a Storage Yard should and shouldn't accept and to control the quantities of each item. Special Orders can also prevent unwanted goods from being delivered to the Storage Yard.

Bazaars

Bazaars are the last link in the chain of getting food

Bazaar

and commodities to people. They are the linchpin to the city's distribution system, and without them the efforts of industries and food producers will be for naught. Bazaars deliver needed supplies to citizens' houses. Residents never interact directly with Storage Yards or Granaries.

Bazaar workers, however, do interact directly with Storage Yards and Granaries to procure needed goods from these locations on behalf of citizens. Each Bazaar employs two buyers: one to buy commodities from Storage Yards, the other to buy food from Granaries. Food buyers can only go to Granaries for supplies; goods buyers can only go to Storage Yards.

Each Bazaar buyer can carry more than one item at time, though. For example, if her Bazaar needs both grain and pomegranates, the food buyer can pick up both foods.

When a Bazaar buyer has picked up supplies, she makes her way back to the Bazaar with a train of helpers in tow. The helpers carry items back to the Bazaar, and the more of them you see, the more supplies she has. Info-click on the Bazaar buyer to see specifically what she is bringing back to the Bazaar.

Bazaars also employ traders to bring the food and goods to the populace. Traders sell whatever commodities the Bazaar has on hand, whether food or good. Houses are supplied with items from the Bazaar when the trader walks by. As she passes each house, the trader also finds out what the citizens in the neighborhood want next and reports back to the buyers so that they can procure the appropriate supplies. If citizens aren't demanding food or a certain good, Bazaar buyers will not purchase it.

To build a Bazaar, click the Storage and Distribution Structures button in the Control Panel. Bazaars need employees and road access.

Bazaar Special Orders

By default, buyers try to procure the commodities the citizens they serve want. To exert more control over the city's Bazaars, you can issue Special Orders.

Info-click on a Bazaar, then click the Special Orders button. You will see a list of all the commodities the Bazaar is trading. Clicking on each item will give you the option of telling the Bazaar to buy or not to buy the item.

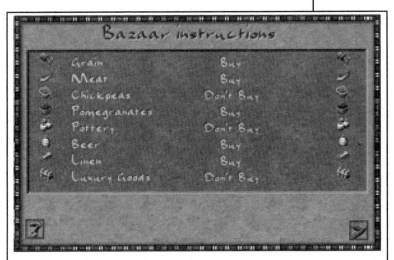

Bazaar Special Orders. Click on the button next to each item to tell the Bazaar whether or not to buy it.

Planning an Efficient Distribution System

The Storage Yard, the Granary and the Bazaar are the basic components of your city's distribution system. Understanding how these three structures interrelate will help you keep your citizens supplied with the food and goods they want. Meeting your citizens' material needs leads to better-quality housing, which leads to an increased Prosperity Rating and allows you to collect more taxes. Keep the following tips in mind as you plan your city to ensure that housing receives a steady supply of the food and goods they need.

Build Bazaars Near Storage Yards and Granaries. Keeping your city's Bazaars well supplied will go a long way to keeping citizens' material wants in check. The best way to keep the city's Bazaars bustling with commodities is to place them near a Granary and a Storage Yard so that buyers can make frequent, short trips.

Use Special Orders to Keep Outlying Storage Yards and Granaries Supplied. As your city expands, you should build Storage Yards and Granaries in outlying areas to keep the Bazaars there stocked with goods. These outlying Storage Yards and Granaries will most likely have difficulty procuring supplies unless you use Special Orders. If you tell outlying Granaries and Storage Yards to "Get" items, cart pushers will issue forth to retrieve the stuff from storage facilities that have some. Enabling the "Get" order does not prevent buyers from taking commodities from Granaries or Storage Yards.

Deliverymen always bring goods to the closest Storage Yard or Granary that can accept their load. Outlying Storage Yards and Granaries may never have supplies delivered to them unless they have been given special orders.

Plan Specialized Storage Yards. If you have built a Storage Yard for the sole purpose of supplying Bazaars with the goods they need, consider using Special Orders to tell the Storage Yard to specialize only in goods for the home. Set the Storage Yard's orders to "Don't Accept" for goods citizens can't use, like weapons, wood, etc. This prevents the Storage Yard from being clogged with items that people deem useless.

Carefully Plan Roads. If there are well-supplied Granaries and Storage Yards near a given Bazaar, it probably won't have a problem keeping food and goods on the shelves. The Bazaar may still have a problem getting these supplies to housing, however, if the city's roads are not laid out well.

The trader is responsible for bringing supplies from the Bazaar to housing. The trader is a roamer (see page 45), and does not follow a set path. Every time she encounters an intersection, she must choose which way to go, and she won't choose the same way every time. The more intersections she comes across, the less predictable her path becomes. And, as the trader is off wandering around the city, housing that needs the goods and foods she provides will go without, and they will devolve.

To keep traders on the straight and narrow, try not to build too many intersections in the city. Another good tool for controlling traders is the Roadblock (see page 109). When a trader — or any other roamer — encounters a Roadblock, she turns around and heads in the other direction. The Roadblock helps prevent traders from wandering off into the industrial or other non-residential sections of the city.

If citizens are not supplied with the food and goods they want, build more Bazaars. As housing develops and evolves, it grows more spacious, and more residents can call it home. Be sure to build more Bazaars as more people move into a neighborhood.

Be patient. Setting up a distribution system is a long process, and it can take time for the system to work properly.

Goods from Near and Far
Ahket, 12th year of Ramesses
Mid-afternoon

Dear Journal,

It was time to deal with the matter at hand. I had been charged with conducting a successful trade mission to Egypt on behalf of my homeland. While Syria is a beautiful land that provides much for its people, our crops are not always reliable. The rain is unpredictable, and many years our harvest is paltry. We look to Egypt to supplement our stocks, offering her the things she lacks.

I went to the Storage Yard and was pleased to see that thieves had left our stocks alone. On this trip, we brought ivory, wine and weapons for trade. I visited the overseer of trade, one of Pharaoh's closest advisors, to strike the deal. In exchange for our fine goods, we received valuable papyrus and an enormous amount of grain that will go far in feeding our people. My business com-

Trade

Few Egyptian cities are completely self-sufficient. Most lack the ability to produce a necessary food or good. To adequately provide for its citizens, a city must trade with others to procure some items it needs (see page 92).

The financial benefit for the city can be great, too. Chances are, a city will make much more money from exporting goods than from taxation.

Opening a Trade Route

Before your city can reap the benefits of healthy trade

---

plete, I returned to Khmunhotep's house to bid him and his family farewell. Imagine my pleasure when Khmunhotep graciously invited me to stay a while. I gratefully accepted his offer, and made the necessary arrangements.

To properly thank Khmunhotep and Nefernetka for their generosity, I stopped by the local Bazaar to find them a present. The Bazaar was teeming with activity. Traders had set their wares out, and local residents were examining the goods, offering grain, linen and other items in exchange. My first stop was at the brewer's stand. To slake my thirst, I bought some beer. The beer was freshly brewed, and the ingredients used for flavoring floated on top. Luckily, the mug has a straw with a filter attached so that I didn't swallow the sediment along with the tasty brew.

I made my way through the booths offering linen, pomegranates, figs and pottery until I found the jeweler's booth. I found a beautiful beaded collar and offered some ivory in exchange. After striking my bargain, I returned to Khmunhotep's home, happy that I would be able to stay longer in Egypt and see more of this fascinating land.

relations, you must first open a trade route. To find out which cities are willing to engage in trade, click on the World Map button on the Control Panel. A map of the world appears with other cities clearly marked. Cities willing to trade with your city are flying a flag.

World Map Button

Click on one of the cities flying a flag to see which items and in what quantities its merchants want to trade. The quantities listed is show that particular city's supply or demand for the year. These amounts can fluctuate with changing situations, but once your city buys or sells the specified amount for a certain item, it cannot deal in that commodity with that particular trade partner for the rest of the year.

Beneath the list of items is a button with the price for opening the trade route. Click on this button to authorize the expenditure from the city's treasury and to open the trade route.

Importing and Exporting

Once you've opened a trade route, tell your Overseer of Commerce to import or export a commodity. The Overseer of Commerce's screen lists all the commodities available to the city, whether through the city's own industries or through importation. Next to each item is the amount currently stored in the city, followed by the trade status of the item. The Overseer of Commerce tells you if an item can be imported or exported. Click on one of these items, and a screen pops up describing the status of that particular industry in your city. Click one of the top buttons to begin trading a commodity.

Importing. Once you have told your Overseer of

Commerce to import an item, you have two options: you can set your own import guidelines or allow the Overseer to do so. When you set a specific import guideline, the city will continue to import the item as long as it has less than the specified amount stored in its Storage Yards. If you let the Overseer of Commerce set his own guidelines, he'll consider the city's needs for the items on an ongoing basis and import an appropriate amount as needed.

Exporting. Much of the time, the same commodities you export are valued by your citizens as well. To keep your citizens happy, be sure to keep an adequate supply of the commodities you are exporting in the city's Storage Yards. You can

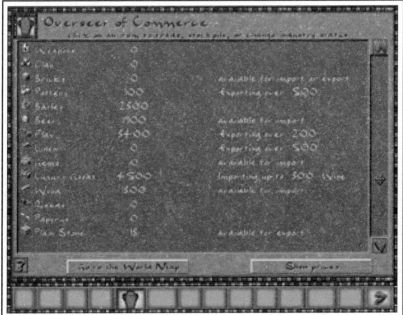

Overseer of Commerce's Screen. The Overseer of Commerce's screen show you wealth of information regarding goods and foods available to your city.

either set a specific amount that should be kept in the Storage Yards or let the Overseer of Commerce determine how much of an item should be kept on hand; then, any surplus items will be exported.

Once you have told the Overseer of Commerce to begin trading a certain item, its trade status will be updated in the Overseer of Commerce's screen. The screen shows which items are being imported and exported. It also shows whether you have set your own trade guidelines or if you have left these decisions up to your Overseer of Commerce.

Sometimes, you can either import or export a commodity, giving you more flexibility as you plan your industries. Deciding whether to import or export a commodity depends upon your goals. If you want to bolster the city's income, then devote the labor needed to produce the commodity and export it. If you want to use the city's labor for another purpose, then import the commodity. You can never import and export the same item at the same time.

A good way to make money, however, is to import a raw material and export a finished product. Manufacturing products from imported raw materials is the best way to make money, and no other source of income will match the potential revenue generated by manufacturing.

Sea and River Trade
Some of the city's trade partners come by water. Great trading vessels float down the Nile, but they won't do your city any good if they don't have a place to dock. Build a Dock on the coastline for these barges to moor.

To function properly, Docks must also have road access and labor. Once a trade ship has docked, cart pushers from the Dock busily unload commodities and bring them to the city's Storage Yards, and then load any goods the city is exporting to this partner and bring them back to the Dock. It's a good idea to build a Storage Yard near your Dock to shorten the cart pushers' journeys.

Commodity Pricing

Your Overseer of Commerce knows the going rate for commodities throughout the world. To see how much items sell or can be purchased for, click on the Show Prices button on the Overseer's screen. Trade status is replaced with price information. The prices shown are per transaction. Click the button again to return to the trade status screen.

When you visit your Overseer of Commerce, you'll notice that buyers pay more for a commodity than sellers receive. Merchants incur expenses transporting items for sale and make up the difference by charging buyers more than sellers receive for items. Luxury goods are an excellent example of the difference between the buyer's price and the seller's price. Because it is so dangerous to transport luxury goods, traders charge a large sum to those wishing to buy them. For the same reason, they pay a small price to those wishing to sell them.

Municipal Functions

Residents have many expectations of their city. They expect to feel safe and to have their homes protected from fire. They also expect city officials to beautify surroundings by planting Gardens, improving roads and erecting Statues.

These benefits, however, do come at a price. Residents also expect their government to levy taxes. While money earned from exporting commodities will likely be the city's primary source of income, tax money nevertheless is an important contributor to any city's coffers.

The Municipal Structures Button

Click on the Municipal Structures button to see all the services a city can offer its citizens, as well as all the means of making them pay for these services.

Constables and Magistrates

Most citizens are content to live peaceable lives. When they have complaints about a city, they voice them calmly or find greener pastures elsewhere. A few, however, express their displeasure through acts of crime. A sizable force of constables and magistrates will help keep the disgruntled at bay.

Constables work out of Police Stations, and magistrates work out of Courthouses. Both these buildings need road access and a supply of labor. Once these buildings are operational, you will see constables walking their beats, and magistrates strolling through the city's neighborhoods. Info-click on these buildings to see if they have full employment and to see what their employees are doing.

Police Station

At the Bazaar
Proyet, 12th year of Ramesses
Morning

Dear Journal,

Today I went to the Bazaar again, this time with Nefernetka. Nefernetka usually does not go to the Bazaar herself, but relies on the traders that work their way through the neighborhoods. But, today we went to the Bazaar ourselves, I think because Nefernetka wanted to be sure to entertain me.

We stopped by a weaver's booth, where the finest linen was set out for examination. The best linen is the thinnest, and indeed this weaver must be well know for her skill because I could see right through some of her cloth. While we were admiring her linen, a commotion erupted behind us. A small monkey, biting for all he was worth, was firmly latched on to the ankle of a man trying to steal a small piece of jewelry. Alerted by the cries, a constable came over to address matters. The woman at the weaver's booth, shaking her head, said, "That's the second time this month that Meryptah has been caught stealing. Last time, the magistrate let him off with 50 blows. He won't be so lenient this time."

After we returned home, I went out to the lovely garden next to Khmunhotep and Nefernetka's house. The garden is replete with sacred lotus blossoms, chrysanthemums and irises. In the center is a lovely statue, flanked by sycamore trees. Trees are rare in Egypt and considered to be sacred residences of the gods.

When constables and magistrates pass by a house, they reduce the likelihood that a criminal will emerge from that house. Keep in mind, though, that constables and magistrates do not follow a set route. They roam the city's streets, and, like other roaming walkers, every time they encounter an intersection they must decide which way to go. See page 51 for more on walkers who roam the city.

Courthouse

Courthouses serve the additional function of storing part of your city's treasury. For more on money in your city, see page 102.

City Sentiment and Crime

Poor City Sentiment is caused when citizens' basic needs are not met. Factors contributing to poor City Sentiment include low wages, high taxes, not enough food and not enough jobs. Social inequality also worsens citizens' moods. Residents become upset if they are paying taxes while others are getting off scott free, or if they are denied services that others in the city have.

When citizens become angry enough, they turn to crime. Their aim is to steal money, either from the city's treasury or from your family savings. To see which houses are likely to spawn thieves, use the Risks: Crime Overlay (see page 204). When viewing this overlay, the city's houses are replaced with columns; the higher the column, the more likely it is that the house will set a criminal loose on the city.

Once a criminal hits the streets, magistrates are power-less to stop him. Constables, however, can apprehend and subdue criminals before they strike. Crime will be averted if a constable encounters a criminal on the city's streets. Providing for your citizens' basic needs to maintain high City Sentiment, though, is the best way to prevent crime.

Other Security Issues

City Defense. Constables try to defend the city from any threat. If the city is invaded, constables will do their best to defeat the foe. They are not, however, equipped with deadly weapons, nor are they schooled in the art of war. Defeating an enemy army is a tall order for constables, but it is a feat the constables can accomplish if there is a tremendous number of them engaged in the fight.

Animal Predators. Similarly, if animals attack the city's inhabitants, constables will step in to help. Animal predators, though, are quite fierce, and it may take more than one constable to subdue them. Dangerous animals include crocodiles, hyenas and hippopotamuses. Military solutions are usually the best defense against animals. A company of soldiers or javelins thrown from towers can make quick work of the animal predators.

Structural Flaws

Large structures, like Storage Yards, mines, Granaries, Temples, and Temple Complexes, are prone to collapse. Architects patrolling your streets repair structural flaws before disaster strikes. Architects are based in Architect's posts, and info-clicking on this building tells you if it is operational and how many employees it has. Once the building is functional, architects begin inspecting buildings for damage.

You can check to see if a particular building has a risk of collapse by using the Risks: Damage Overlay (see page 206). If you notice that a certain building or group of buildings has a high risk of collapse, you may want to place an Architect's post nearby to ensure that an architect provides his services (see page 51 for more on roaming walkers).

Architect's post

Collapse can have catastrophic effects. If a Granary or Storage Yard collapses, any food or goods stored there will be lost.

Fire Prevention

Some buildings in your city are prone to fire. Likely candidates include run-down housing and industry buildings like potters. If you do nothing to stop it, fire can spread through the city, destroying whole sections at one time. To prevent this, build Firehouses near buildings that are likely to catch fire. To find out which buildings could go up in smoke, use the Risks: Fire overlay. The Fire Overlay shows you where the highest risk of fire is, indicating where you may need more Firehouses.

Firehouse

Palaces

One of the most majestic buildings in the city is the Palace. This building is a physical reminder of Egypt's power.

A city can have only one Palace, and the building serves as its seat of government. Without this important meeting place, the city cannot collect taxes. The Palace, however, does not send out its own tax collectors. You need to build Tax Collectors' offices (see page 104) to take in what the city is owed.

In addition to road access and labor, at least one part of the Palace must be on grassland to supply it with ground water. High ranking officials from Egypt and abroad stay in the Palace when visiting the city.

The Palace also provides an "at-a-glance" look at your ratings. When you hold the cursor over the building, a balloon listing your ratings, the tax rate and the unemployment rate appears.

You can also set your city's tax rate by info-clicking on the Palace. On the pop-up panel, the tax rate is listed. Click the buttons to the right of the tax rate adjust it up or down.

If the city is fortunate enough to have Gold Mines nearby (see page 70), the Palace accepts the gold ore and converts it into cash.

Palaces come in three different sizes: Village, Town and City. In each city, only one of these sizes will be available to build, depending on the rank you have attained.

Taxes and Money
Once the Palace is built, the city can begin collecting taxes.

When your city is new and its industries are in their infancies, taxes are essential to keeping the city solvent. Even when trade revenue picks up, charging citizens taxes can provide a sizable supplement to the city's income.

Setting a Tax Rate

By default, the tax rate is set at 9 percent. To change this rate, either info-click on the city's Palace or visit the Overseer of the Treasury. Setting the city's tax rate at the Palace is described on the previous page.

The Overseer of the Treasury provides you with a wealth of information that will help you decide at what level to set the tax rate. In addition to listing the tax rate itself, he tells you what percentage of the population is currently registered for the tax (that is, how many are visited by tax collectors), and how much revenue is generated. He also knows how much more money the city would earn if every citizen was registered for the tax.

With this information, you can decide what to do about the city's tax rate. If the city isn't earning enough from taxes, the answer may be to build more Tax Collectors' offices. Use the Administration: Tax Income Overlay (see page 208) to see which neighborhoods aren't paying their fair share.

Raising taxes can be a good idea if the city is in debt and needs a quick influx of money. Increasing taxes, however, is not a good long-term solution to the city's money problems. A high tax rate has a dramatic negative effect on City Sentiment, and citizens will not tolerate high taxes for long. Many of them will move from your city, draining your city of its work force. Other citizens may turn to crime (see page 47). Be judicious when raising the city's tax rate, and carefully watch your citizens' reactions.

Lowering taxes, on the other hand, pleases your citizens. They will praise your name in the streets as a wise and benevolent ruler.

Tax Collectors

Citizens do expect to pay taxes, but they need a little prodding. Tax collectors go door to door, assessing what each household can afford and making sure citizens are paying their fair share.

Tax Collectors' office

Tax collectors work out of Tax Collectors' offices. These buildings need road access and labor in order to operate. The city must also have a Palace (see page 101) before you can build Tax Collectors' offices. If the Palace is destroyed, the Tax Collectors' offices will remain, but they will no longer send out tax collectors.

Build Tax Collectors' offices anywhere you have houses to ensure that most citizens are registered for the tax. Sometimes, it may not be advantageous to have a tax collector patrolling in particularly poor areas of your city. Your poorest citizens will not owe much in taxes, and the amount your tax collectors collect from them may not outweigh the expense of building a Tax Collector post and paying its staff. Your poor citizens' lives are hard enough; you might choose not to add to their burden by taking their meager savings.

Also be sure to tax all the city's residents fairly. If only about half of the city's inhabitants are visited by a tax collector, they will become disgruntled quickly, which could lower City Sentiment and cause people to turn to a life of crime. Fairness is important to Egyptians, and they want to be sure that people in similar stations as themselves are also paying tax.

Tax Collectors' offices, like the Palace and Courthouses, each store a portion of your city's funds.

The City Treasury

The money the city makes from collecting taxes, mining gold, receiving gifts and exporting goods is stored in vaults located in the Palace, the Tax Collectors' offices and the Courthouses. The Palace has the largest vault and can store the most money. Each Courthouse can store about half of what a Palace can store. Tax Collectors' offices can store about one-third of what the Palace stores. If one of these buildings is destroyed by invaders, some of the city's funds will be plundered. If you demolish one of these buildings yourself, the city's treasury will not be affected.

The City's Funds and Debt

Your Overseer of the Treasury keeps a running tally of the treasury's balance and provides the previous year's information for comparison's sake. He uses several line items in his assessment of your city's fortunes. By visiting him, you will be able to see the city's sources of income. You'll also be able to see where the city's money goes.

If you spend too much, the city will obviously go into debt. The Kingdom will extend a credit line of up to 5,000 debens, but this comes with a price. The Kingdom charges a sizable interest rate, so paying the city's debt off quickly is very important. The city must

---

Pharaoh's Palace and Industrial Life
Proyet, 12th year of Ramesses
Morning
Dear Journal

Early this morning, Khmunhotep and I made our way to the center of town to a colossal Mansion. It is one of Pharaoh's many homes, and a great fortune is locked in its vaults. On the side of the Palace is a large, artificial lake. Pharaoh and his favorite wife sail their barge, Amun Gleams, there. The Palace is also home to 317 Hittite women, whom Pharaoh received as part of a dowry for marrying a Hittite princess.

From the palace, we headed for the industrial district. Khmunhotep is familiar with my fascination for the way things work and knew I would enjoy a visit to some of the town's manufacturers. A cacophony greeted us: the pounding of the papyrus makers intermingled with the chatter of the linen weavers. Waves of heat emanated from the fiery kiln at the potters' workshop, and the potter barked orders to his assistant, insisting that he turn the wheel faster. The assistant's whine, 'I can't turn this any faster,' added to the noise. Distinct smells wafted through the air, particularly the hearty scent of malted barley being made into beer.

make these interest payments every year, even if it has to borrow more money to do so. If the city owes more than 5,000 debens, you won't be able to build any new structures, but the city will be able to incur even more debt due to interest payments. Watch the city's funds carefully, and do all you can to avoid debt.

If the city incurs debt, others in Egypt may begin to question your abilities to successfully govern a city. Debt damages your Kingdom Rating (see page 194), and the city may be attacked if your Kingdom Rating sinks low enough. Unless you have an extremely large, well-trained military to defeat these armies and navies, the city will be destroyed and you will fail the mission.

Mansions

Because of your family's importance, you are allowed to build a Mansion using funds from the city's treasury. Your residence is a grand structure, and neighboring citizens swell with pride when they pass by your home. In addition to providing a place for respite, your residence stores your family savings (see below). In fact, you cannot draw a salary until you have built a Mansion.

The Mansion must have road access. It does not require labor, but, because it is your home, it must be built on grassland to supply it with ground water. At least one part of the Mansion must be placed over green grass.

As your family becomes more prominent, you will be able to build bigger Mansions. The sizes of Mansions are Personal, Family and Dynasty.

Your Salary

All your toiling to build a great Egyptian city does not go unrewarded. You are granted a salary based on your rank. As long as you have a Mansion, you can earn an income. If you think you are worth more (or less) than what you are paid, you can adjust your own salary accordingly. Keep in mind that others in the Kingdom may not look too kindly on you if you pay yourself a hefty salary. They will question your dedication to the Kingdom, and your Kingdom Rating (see page 194) may suffer the consequences of your ego.

The Political Overseer (see page 198) saves your salary for your family and keeps track of you family savings balance. Family savings is stored in your residence and usually is passed down to your heirs. If the central government breaks down, signifying the end of a Period, your family savings are lost.

Spending Your Family Savings

There are two ways to spend your family savings: you can send gifts to the people of Egypt or give to the city.

To maintain a good reputation in the Kingdom, the most important thing you can do is establish a thriving, profitable city. Of course, those who donate gifts to Egypt are thought of very highly. Be forewarned, though, that people in the Kingdom bore quickly, so your gifts must become fancier and more expensive over time. If they don't, others might think you are getting cheap, and your standing in the Kingdom could decrease.

To send a gift to the Kingdom, visit your Political

Overseer and click on the button "Send a Gift." You have three choices of gifts to send, each one increasing on the previous one's lavishness. Consider how much your family has saved, and choose a gift accordingly.

If the city is about to go in the red, you may want to supplement the city's funds with your family's savings. Debt is not looked upon lightly in the Kingdom (see page 194). If your funds can save the city from incurring debt, you'd be well served to contribute it to the city's coffers.

Your Political Overseer will manage the process of giving from your family savings. Visit him, and click on the "Give to City" button to begin the transaction. Specify an amount, and click on the "Give to City" button. Your Political Overseer will ensure that the city's treasury receives the funds.

Roadblocks

Roadblocks help you control the paths roaming walkers take. When walkers who roam the city encounter

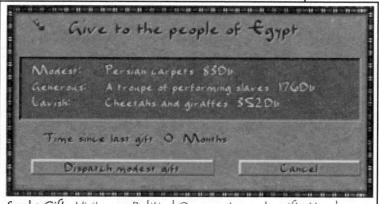

Send a Gift. Visit your Political Overseer to send a gift. You have three gifts from which to choose.

Road Block

a Roadblock, they turn around. Roadblocks do not affect destination walkers. See page 50 for more on walkers.

Build a Roadblock anywhere that your roaming walkers don't need to go, for example, on the road to your industrial areas. Be wary, though, of isolating areas entirely from walkers who roam the city. The same Roadblock that keeps a trader from the Bazaar from wandering into the industrial sector also turns back architects, fire marshals and constables. It also stops labor recruiters from walking from the industrial area to your housing sector where they find employees.

Water Crossings

Egypt wouldn't survive without the Nile, but the river does cause an interesting wrinkle in city planning. Luckily, you can access both fertile shores of the Nile by building water crossings.

Bridges

A Bridge is an inexpensive way to cross a small body of water. It can only cross a short expanse of water, and no ships can pass under it, including fishing boats and warships. Use a Bridge if the distance to be spanned is small and if there's no boat traffic on the body of water.

Bridge

Bridges must be built on a smooth section of coastline, and there must be a corresponding smooth section of coastline on the opposite shore. If a bridge may be built on the location you choose, you will see a green "ghost" of the bridge as you try to place it. If the bridge cannot be built, you will see a red square.

Ferries

Water can also be crossed with ferries. Ferries are much more versatile than Bridges and do not block water traffic.

To provide ferry service to the city, two Ferry Landings must be built. Like other coastal structures, Ferry Landings must be built on a smooth section of coast. As with other structures, you will know if you have picked an appropriate place to build your Ferry Landing if you see a green ghost of the building. After you place the first Landing, you will see green squares on the opposite coast. You may build the other Ferry Landing on any of these green squares.

Both Ferry Landings must have staff and road access before either will operate, so you'll probably need to designate some housing on the far side of the river as soon as you build the Landings. Ferry masters provide their own boats, so the services of a Shipwright are not needed.

Once you have built the Ferry Landings, emigrants and immigrants can cross the water. Because they use their own boats, emigrants and immigrants can use Ferry Landings even if the buildings do not have road access or labor. Ferry Landings, however, do need road access and labor to carry other people back and forth.

All destination walkers can use the ferries (see page 50 for more on destination walkers). This includes buyers from the Bazaar on their way to storage facilities and entertainers making their way from performer

Should your water crossing be damaged, it is important to rebuild it as soon as possible. Residents and industry cut off from the main road (the road that existed when you began building your city) will shortly die if they remain boxed in.

schools to entertainment venues. Soldiers can also use ferries if they are going from the Recruiter or Academy to their fort. Companies of soldiers, however, must use military transport ships to cross the river (see page 182).

Each Ferry Landing has one ferry boat. Both boats wait until one boat has four passengers before making their crossings. The four passengers can be any combination of destination walkers. If a delivery man with goods is one of the passengers, the goods he is transporting are also ferried across the river. A ferry boat will set sail before it has a full load of passengers if enough time passes.

If there is no more room on a ferry boat, people will patiently wait in line until space opens up. If you notice long lines at the Ferry Landings, consider building additional Ferry Landings.

Should one of the Ferry Landings be destroyed, you can rebuild it by selecting "Ferry Landing" from the Municipal Structures: Water Crossings menu, then clicking on the Landing that has not been destroyed. When you do so, the familiar green squares again appear on the opposite shore, and you can rebuild the other Ferry Landing. The city's treasury will be charged

only for the cost of one of the buildings.

Beautification

No matter how many goods and services the city provides, its inhabitants won't feel that they live in a great city unless their surroundings are attractive. Beautification structures give a city character and make citizens feel that all their hard work has a purpose. Beautification also has a positive impact on a neighborhood's desirability. For more on desirability, see page 42

Gardens

Gardens provide a place for your citizens to relax after a hard day's work, and their lushness provides shelter from the hot Egyptian sun. All citizens like to have Gardens nearby; some may demand them.

Garden

To plan a Garden, choose them from the Beautification tab under Municipal Structures. Gardens become more impressive the more space you devote to them. While citizens appreciate small Gardens, they like large Gardens the best.

While gardens do provide a place for your citizens to relax, they do not produce any food.

Gardens do not need road access or labor and cannot collapse or catch fire. Walker who do not need to walk on roads, like fire marshals on their way to extinguish a fire, can cut through Gardens.

Plazas

Plazas are intricately tiled roads. They can only be built on roads that citizens have already paved (see page 40 for more on paved roads). They add a touch of quality to your city's neighborhoods.

Plaza

To build them, click on the Plazas button in the Municipal Structures: Beautification list. Then, click on the paved road. You can place Plazas one section at a time, or drag the mouse to place Plazas over a large stretch of road.

Plazas do not change the road's carrying capacity or walkers' speed of travel on them, and they do not require labor.

Statues

Statues are reminders of everything that makes Egyptians proud.

Statues come in three sizes: small, medium and large. Each size offers two options. After you have selected the size of Statue you want, hold the mouse over the location you've chosen and press "R" on the keyboard until the style of statue you want is facing the direction you like. Then, click the mouse button to place the statue.

The larger the Statue, the greater its effect on desirability. Statues do not need road access and cannot collapse or catch fire.

Religion and the Gods

The gods are credited with much of what is good in Egypt. They influence all aspects of an Egyptian city, from the Nile's floods to the success of its industry to the health of its citizens. If you appease them, they will reward you. Should you fail to pay proper respect, beware. The gods act swiftly to remind you where your attention should lie.

The Gods of Egypt

Five major gods are revered in Egypt, but not all are necessarily worshipped in every city. While some cities worship all five gods, others may worship only one or two. Each deity influences a specific aspect of life.

 Osiris. Osiris is the God of Agriculture and the Nile Flood. Keeping him appeased will help ensure that the Nile floods its banks predictably. Ignoring him could wreak havoc with the annual flood, making it particularly destructive or, worse, causing it not to happen at all.

Ra. As God of the Kingdom, Ra influences your standing within Egypt. He can affect trade and other Kingdom-related matters.

 Ptah. Ptah, God of Craftsmen, watches over industry in your city. He can make your industries more productive, or he can destroy them.

Seth. As god of Destruction, Seth is most interested in tools of destruction. His main area of influence, then, is your military. He can bestow protection on your soldiers or heartlessly strike them down, depending on how well you treat him.

 Bast. Bast is the Goddess of the Home and touches your citizens' lives by affecting their health and well-being. If she smiles upon the city, she will help make sure citizens are well fed and satisfied. Incur her wrath, and she will destroy people's homes or their health.

Patron Gods and Local Deities

Most cities have a patron god. This god pays special attention to the city, but also requires more attention from it. Cities might also worship local deities. While they may lack the stature of the city's patron god, local deities still punish or reward a city based on its behavior.

You must do more to keep the city's patron god appeased. The patron god expects to have more Temples and Shrines dedicated to him or her than the deities in your city. To do great honor to the patron god, build a Temple Complex for him or her.

Local deities know that they won't receive as much attention as the patron god, but each local deity demands equal treatment to other local deities.

To find out if the gods are satisfied with the city, visit

the Overseer of the Temples. He knows which gods are worshiped by the citizens and how each god is feeling towards the city.

Religious Buildings

The best way to keep the gods appeased is to make sure plenty of buildings are dedicated to them. There are several different buildings from which to choose, as you will see when you click on the "Religious Structures" button on the Control Panel.

Religious Structures
Button

> **Shrines.** Shrines are the simplest religious structures you can build. They do not require road access, but they do need to be within two spaces of the road to receive services from fire marshals and architects. A Shrine's sole purpose is to please the god to which it is dedicated. While they have a positive effect on a neighborhood's desirability, they do not provide citizens access to religion. Shrines do not employ workers.

Shrine

> **Temples.** Temples are much larger structures than Shrines, and active worship of the gods occurs inside them. When a Temple is built, you must dedicate it to a particular god. Once the Temple is fully operational, you will see priests on your city's streets bringing religion to your people.

Temple

> **Temple Complexes.** Generally, you can build a Temple Complex only for the patron god of the city. Sometimes, you can build a Temple Complex to a local deity if that deity is particularly important. A city can only have one Temple Complex at a time, so be careful before you build one to a local deity. The patron god could become quite

upset, and the city will likely feel his or her anger.

Temple Complexes are costly, but worth the expense as their mere presence provides benefits to the city.

Temples Complexes, Altars and Oracles

Once you place the Temple Complex, you can build additional structures onto it. These are called an Oracle and an Altar. Each Altar and Oracle is dedicated to a different, minor god, enabling your city to honor three gods with one building. While the gods honored with Oracles and Altars are of smaller stature, they still bring benefits to your city.

Osiris' Temple Complex

When you build a Temple Complex for Osiris, he looks to the Nile to reward the city. The Nile is more likely to have good floods when there is a Temple Complex for Osiris in the city. You can build the following additions onto Osiris' Temple Complex:

Altar of Sebek, God of Fertility. Sebek grants priests of Osiris the power to stretch the city's supplies of food and goods. As priests of Osiris walk through your city, the people in the houses they pass are suddenly satisfied with less.

Oracle of Min, God of Regeneration. When your city honors Min with an Oracle, he blesses the city by speeding the regrowth of trees and reeds, increasing the rate at which prey animals reproduce and improving the yield from fishing and hunting.

Ra's Temple Complex

Ra smiles upon the city when it has dedicated a Temple Complex to him, and he rewards the city by making sure others in the Kingdom smile upon it. Building a Temple Complex for Ra increases your Kingdom Rating and, should the city find itself in debt, allows you to get away with paying a

---

A visit to the Temple
Proyet, 12th year of Ramesses
Afternoon
Dear Journal,

Khmunhotep took me to a temple dedicated to Ra. This great temple was absolutely beautiful with engravings and paintings covering its surface. Two great obelisks flanked the temple's front entrance. The obelisks were capped with gold that mirrors the sun's brilliant rays. Khmunhotep and I purchased some food and left it as an offering. We entered the courtyard and joined the throngs of people who had come there to pay homage to the god. While there, Khmunhotep asked the

god whether his son would be a successful scribe. The god replied in the affirmative, and Khmunhotep left the temple a happy man.

lower interest rate. Building an Altar and Oracle onto the Temple Complex of Ra helps you manage the city's affairs:

Altar of Ma'at, Goddess of Justice. Through priests of Ra, Ma'at bestows a calming effect on your city. As they pass by houses, they lower the likelihood that the house will unleash a criminal. The simple presence of the Altar reduces the city's overall risk of crime breaking out.

Oracle of Horus, God of the Pharaohs. This Oracle increases citizens' dedication to Pharaoh and to the Kingdom, encouraging them to accept a lower wage without affecting their mood.

Ptah's Temple Complex

When you build him a Temple Complex, Ptah speeds the production of many of your city's industries, including Gold Mines, Copper Mines Gemstone Mines, Clay Pits, Shipwrights, Jewelers and Weavers. The Altar and Oracle in Ptah's Temple Complex speed the production of other industries and improves educators' abilities:

Altar of Amon, God of the Sun. Honored by your attention, Amon spurs quarries, Wood Cutters, and Brickworks to work more quickly.

Oracle of Thoth, God of Wisdom and Learning. Thoth's goal is to bring the light of learning to as many people as possible. When you build an Oracle of Thoth, librarians and teachers use less papyrus to educate the city's inhabitants.

Seth's Temple Complex

When a city has a Temple Complex dedicated to him, Seth instills a fierce will in the city's soldiers, granting them more experience, protecting them in battle. The additions to Seth's Temple Complex are:

Altar of Anubis, God of Death. Anubis gives easier access to eternal life for citizens in the city. With his blessing, embalmers need less linen to prepare bodies for eternity.

Oracle of Sekhmet, Goddess of War. Sekhmet endows priests of Seth with the power to reduce the risk of crime in the houses that

Temple Complex. While costly, Temple Complexes provide tremendous benefits to your city.

they pass and to apprehend criminals in the city.

Bast's Temple

Building a Temple to Bast brings good fortune to any city. Bast helps keep citizens happy by making them satisfied with less. As a result of her benevolence, the rate at which your citizens consume food and goods is reduced, and the effects of entertainers, educators and health providers last longer. Her sister goddesses also improve life for your citizens:

> **Altar of Isis, Goddess of Healing.** Through priestesses of Bast, Isis lays her healing hands on the city's populace, removing plagued walkers from the streets and cleansing any infected houses the priestesses may pass. Isis also takes care to improve your city's overall health.

> **Oracle of Hathor, Goddess of Joy, Love and Festivity.** Hathor, flattered by the Oracle you have built for her, will improve citizens' mood, resulting in a better City Sentiment.

Festivals and Festival Squares

A festival appeases the god to whom it is dedicated and also boosts your citizens' spirits, which results in an improved City Sentiment.

Before you can hold a festival, you must have a Festival Square in your city. Build a Festival Square by clicking on the Religious Structures Icon and choosing it from the list. A Festival Square must be placed over a crossroads intersection, but it does not require labor. Each city can have only one Festival Square.

Once you have built a Festival Square, info-click on it or visit your Overseer of the Temples (see page 202) to order a festival. The Overseer of the Temples knows how long it has been since the last festival in your city, and how long it has been since a festival has been thrown in the honor of each god.

Decide which god you would like to dedicate a festival to and then click on the "Hold a Festival" button. A new screen pops up with pictures of each of the gods worshiped in the city. Specify the one you would like to honor with a festival, then decide how large a festival to throw.

Common festivals are the most economical, but have the least effect on the gods and the city's residents. Lavish festivals are more appreciated by the gods, and your citizens enjoy the revelry these offer. Grand festivals are the most popular with both the gods and your citizens. Beer flows freely at grand festivals, and before you can throw one, there must be enough beer stored in the city's Storage Yards. Your Overseer of the Temples tells you how much is needed. If a god is particularly angry with the city, throwing a grand festival in his or her honor could save the city from a disaster.

Once you have finished the festival plans, the festival occurs after a few months of detailed preparations. Visit the Overseer of the Temples to find out exactly when the festival will occur. When it is time for the festival, Priests from the temple of the honored god make their way towards the Festival Square, along with entertainers and scribes from your wealthier houses.

As governor of the city, you, too, make an appearance at the festival to pay homage to the honored god and mingle with the citizens.

Organizers cannot prepare more than two festivals in any 12 month period. If you have already held two festivals in any given 12 month period, your organizers will accept an order for another festival, but will not be able to begin preparations for it yet. If plans for a festival are already under way, you cannot order a second festival until the first one has taken place.

Monuments

reat leaders are remembered for many reasons. Some are remembered for their great success in battle, others for their sage rule or wise diplomatic relations. The leaders best remembered, however, are those who leave behind a physical reminder of their glory. The larger and more magnificent this reminder, the better.

In Egypt, these lofty reminders take the shape of great monuments. The form of these monuments changes with time. New technology is discovered, and new styles are revered. Most monuments are built from a tremendous amount of raw materials, and all of them need the services of at least one construction guild.

Religious Structures Button

Building Monuments

To successfully complete most missions, you will need to build at least one monument. Some missions will require you to build several. You can build the needed monuments in any order you choose.

Your city's laborers can work on more than one monument at once, and you might be tempted to order them to do so. Be forewarned, however, that such a plan might not be as wise as it first appears. Inefficiency can creep in when stonemasons and block haulers fail to coordinate their work. Peasants might deliver construction materials to one monument site while the stonemasons wait, idle, at the site where they would prefer to work.

This situation frustrates the Overseer of Monuments deeply (see page 203), but it is harder than you would think to reconcile the block haulers' inflexible orders with the stonemasons' independent attitudes. It is best to avoid such conflict altogether by ordering your city's monuments to be built sequentially, rather than simultaneously.

Construction Guilds

To build any of the great monuments that make Egypt famous, you must have construction guilds working in the city. If you will be needing their services, you will see them listed when you click the Industrial Structures button.

Stonemasons' Guild

Each guild is host to skilled construction workers, each of which specialize in working with one material. The guilds need both road access and labor. The types of guilds are:

Carpenters' Guild
Bricklayers' Guild
Stonemasons' Guild

Bricklayers' Guild

Carpenters' Guilds stockpile supplies of wood so that they can respond quickly to construction requests. Stonemasons' Guilds and Bricklayers' Guilds do not keep a store of raw materials on hand; when their services are needed, they wait at the monument for peasants to deliver large sledge loads of brick or stone.

Carpenters' Guild

The most complex monument, the brick-core pyramid, requires services from all three construction guilds. Most monuments will need the efforts of one or two of the guilds.

Work Camps

In addition to providing peasants to work on flood-

plain farms, Work Camps supply the brute force needed to construct a monument. When bricklayers or
stonemasons are ready at the site and Storage Yards
have the needed supplies in stock, a team of peasants
drags a huge sledge full of the required raw material,
either stone or brick, to the monument site.

A Work Camp's first priority is to send peasants to
floodplain farms. If you build enough Work Camps,
though, work on monuments can continue year
round.

Construction Foreman and Overseer of Monuments

The Construction Foreman and Overseer of
Monuments provide you with all the information you
need to know to successfully complete a monument.

Your Overseer of Monuments can tell you what is preventing construction from starting on a monument.
He also manages the dispatch of burial provisions to
any tombs that may require them.

Once construction begins, the Construction Foreman
provides much more detailed information on the project. He keeps a running tally of how much of each
construction material is needed to complete the monument. If construction is not running smoothly, he
can tell you why. To visit the Construction Foreman,
info-click on the monument site.

Placing a Monument

Because of their immense size, some monuments can
be especially difficult to place in your city. For the

largest monuments, you won't be able to see the entire footprint of the structure at one time.

To assess a selected location for a monument, press the "M" key. The monument's footprint will freeze in the spot you selected, and you can move your viewpoint around the city as normally. To place the monument in the selected location, provided it's a viable location, click the mouse button. To continue to look for a suitable spot, press the "M" key again. The monument's footprint will again follow your cursor around your city.

Monuments

Mastabas

Mastabas are the earliest tomb structures to be built in Egypt. They are made entirely of bricks, and the ser-

Mastaba. This small mastaba is under way.

Visiting the Monuments
Proyet, 13th year of Ramesses
Morning

Dear Journal,

Today, I struck out on my own. I had heard much of these Pyramids, the final resting-place of great pharaohs, but couldn't believe what I had been told. One person who had seen them told me that they dwarf everything around them. So, I left the house very early in the morning to sail to Rostja to see for myself.

I hired a man to take me on his boat down to Rostja. When we were well into our journey, I could see the Pyramids in the distance. I thought that we would soon be upon them, but we kept sailing down the river. As we glided along, the Pyramids got bigger and bigger, as did my sense of awe. Finally, the boatsman moored the boat, and we entered the Valley Temple and walked down a long causeway to the base of the Pyramid. It is impossible to exaggerate their size; until I had seen them, I couldn't imagine a structure so huge or so gorgeous. Fine limestone encased the Pyramids, and they glistened in the sun. The biggest Pyramid was built for Khufu who reigned a thousand years before the current pharaoh. My guide told me that as magnificent as the outside of the Pyramids are, the insides are reputed to be even more beautiful. The walls are painted with stories heralding pharaoh's greatness, and hordes of riches are kept in the burial chamber itself for the pharaoh's use in the afterlife.

vices of bricklayers from a Bricklayers' Guild are needed to construct them. Mastabas come in three sizes and always face east.

To build a Mastaba, click on the Religious Structures: Monuments button and choose Mastaba from the monument list. As you move the cursor over the land, you will see the footprint of the building. If the footprint is red, you cannot place the Mastaba in the location you've chosen. If the footprint is green, you have chosen a suitable location. If you are having trouble placing the monument, press the "M" key to freeze the footprint in place (see page 132).

Once you click on a valid location, the corners of the Mastaba are marked with stakes. From this point, peasants and bricklayers take over.

You can watch workers each step of the way as they construct the Mastaba. After peasants clear the land, removing sand and top soil until a solid base is exposed, a team of bricklayers makes their way to the construction site and waits for a delivery of brick. Once there are at least 400 bricks stored in the city's Storage Yards, peasants drag a sledge loaded with the material to the bricklayers at the construction site.

Each load of bricks is enough for one course of one section of the Mastaba. The number of courses and the number of sections in each course varies with the size of the monument.

Info-click on the Mastaba at any time for a progress report on the project.

Pyramids

Pyramids are the largest and most complex structures you will build. They require a large amount of empty land and take years to construct. But, with the right amount of raw materials and brute labor, your Pyramid will soon reach towards the sky.

The most elaborate Pyramids are part of a larger Pyramid Complex. In addition to the Pyramid, the Complex includes a Mortuary Temple, a Valley Temple and a Causeway. At the Mortuary Temple, located on the eastern face of the Pyramid, the deceased is worshiped and offerings are made to ease his existence in the afterlife. The long Causeway connecting the Valley Temple in the east to the Mortuary Temple in the west

Pyramid Construction. This Pyramid has begun Phase II of its construction. Peasants have cleared and leveled the land and the tomb has been cut. Now, stonemasons are awaiting delivery of stone to continue Pyramid construction.

to the world of the dead and mimics the journey of the sun. In the Valley Temple, located on the Nile, the deceased's body is prepared for his journey. Construction workers know exactly how these buildings fit together, so you won't need to worry about placing the individual buildings.

In fact, construction workers, under the direction of the Foreman, know everything about building Pyramids and Pyramid Complexes. Once you choose a location for your monument, construction workers handle the rest, as long as you provide them with what they need.

A Pyramid is built in a few basic but time consuming phases.

Phase I: Preparing the Site

To ensure that the Pyramid stands for thousands of years, peasants must carefully prepare and level the site. To start the peasants on their task, you must first choose a location for the Pyramid.

Choosing a Site. Click on the Religious Structures: Monuments button on the Control Panel. From the list, choose the Pyramid you wish to build. You may have the choice of several sizes or type of Pyramids to build, or you may be offered only one choice. After selecting a Pyramid, point the cursor to the landscape. A footprint of the Pyramid will appear. If this footprint is red, it means that you cannot build in that location. If the footprint is green, then you can place the Pyramid in the location you've chosen. Click the mouse button to assign the Pyramid's location. Once you do, you will see stakes marking the corners of the monument.

Remember, if you are building a Pyramid Complex, the Valley Temple must be adjacent to the water on a straight piece of coastline. Because Pyramid Complexes must be on the west side of the Nile, the Valley Temple must always be to the east of the Pyramid. To help you consider a chosen location, press the "M" key on the keyboard to freeze the monument footprint

You don't have to clear trees or other removable terrain before placing the Pyramid. Peasants will take care of that task. However, if buildings obstruct your chosen Pyramid site, you have to demolish the buildings yourself. Like other buildings, Pyramids can only be placed on stable terrain, and not on sand dunes, rock or marshland.

Leveling the Site. Once the Pyramid has been placed, peasants take over. They clear the land of any trees or meadow and remove sand and top soil until they reach solid stone bedrock. Then, they level the site.

To level the site, peasants first cut grooves into the bedrock and fill the grooves with water. They mark the water's height, and then drain out the water. The peasants cut down the rock to the level of the mark, then fill in the remaining grooves with rubble. The result of the process is a level piece of solid rock on which to build the Pyramid.

In Pyramid Complexes, the site for the Pyramid itself is the only site leveled. The land that the rest of the Complex will occupy does not need to be leveled.

After the site is levelled, peasants cut the tomb that will ultimately house the deceased. The tomb is cut into the center of the Pyramid.

Phase II: Constructing the Pyramid

After the site is prepared, construction workers move in to build the Pyramid, laying stones or bricks.

Pyramids are made mostly of plain stone or bricks. With the exception of Stepped Pyramids, all Pyramids have an outer casing of fine limestone. When they are ready, construction workers from the city's construction guilds move to the Pyramid site and wait for a delivery. Whenever a Storage Yard accumulates the required raw material, peasants load the material on a sledge and drag it to the construction site. As long as your city has enough peasant laborers, the necessary construction guilds and supplies of raw materials, Pyramid construction will continue.

Carpenters also contribute their services to Pyramid construction. They build the ramps that allow peasants and construction workers to scale the sides of the Pyramid. Carpenters use the wood they have on hand at the Carpenters Guild. Ordinary deliverymen from a Storage Yard or Wood Cutter provide the Carpenters Guild with wood.

Pyramids are built block by block. Info-click on the Pyramid to check in with the Construction Foreman. He tells you how many more bricks or blocks of stone are needed to complete the current level of the Pyramid. He also knows how much more is needed to complete the entire monument.

If the Pyramid is part of a Pyramid Complex, construction workers will build the Complex at the same time they build the Pyramid.

Phase III: Finishing the Outer Casing

To finish the Pyramid, stonemasons smooth the outer limestone layer so that the Pyramid glistens white in the sun. No more stone is required for this task. As its name implies, the Stepped Pyramid does not undergo this finishing phase.

Pyramid Types

When Pharaoh Djoser first asks your family to help Vizier Imhotep build a Pyramid, you'll have little idea what to expect. Imhotep describes his vision for a mammoth tomb that reaches toward the sun. As generations pass and forebears pass their knowledge to their successors, the vision of the Pyramid changes. Your family is an active participant in the evolution of the Pyramid, guiding the sacred tomb through the following forms:

Stepped Pyramid. Stepped Pyramids, the first Pyramids built in Egypt, are giant staircases to the sun. They are made entirely of plain stone, although wooden ramps are needed to carry stone up to the higher levels of the Pyramid. To build ramps and lay the stone, you'll need a Carpenters' Guild and a Stonemasons' Guild. Peasants are also needed to pull the huge sledge loads of stone over to the construction site. Once four blocks of plain stone are stored in the Storage Yards, and the stonemasons are ready, peasants will begin their arduous journey to the monument site.

Stepped Pyramids come in five different sizes: small, medium, large, Pyramid Complex and grand Pyramid Complex.

Bent Pyramid. Inspired by the sun, the architects who contrived the Bent Pyramid envisioned a giant obelisk with bent sides, representing one of the sun's warming rays. So that it would shine as brightly as the sun, the sides of the Pyramid were smoothed.

To build a Bent Pyramid, you will need supplies of plain stone and limestone, and peasants from a Work Camp. When four blocks of either plain stone or limestone

Stepped Pyramid. A completed Stepped Pyramid is a welcome addition to any city.

are stored in the Storage Yards, peasants load the stone onto a sledge and drag it over to the construction site. To properly place the stones, the services of the Stonemasons Guild are essential. The Carpenters Guild provides ramps from wood that is delivered to the Carpenters' Guild.

Bent Pyramids come in two sizes.

True Pyramid. With the first True Pyramid comes the perfection of the Pyramid form. The True Pyramid is many things: a path to the sun, a sun's ray and the primordial mound from which all life in Egypt sprung.

The True Pyramid has a plain stone core with a limestone casing that is smoothed and polished. Stonemasons from the Stonemasons' Guild lay the stone and polish the surface, while carpenters from the Carpenters' Guild prepare the ramps necessary for construction as the Pyramid rises higher and higher. When a Storage Yard has accumulated four blocks of stone, peasants drag a sledge loaded with the stone to the monument site to the waiting stonemasons.

The True Pyramid sizes are small, medium, large, Pyramid Complex and grand Pyramid Complex.

Brick-Core Pyramid. Sometimes, plain stone is difficult to obtain, so bricks are used for the core of the Pyramid instead. Brick-core Pyramids are the most complex Pyramids you will build because they require three types of raw materials and three types of construction guilds. You need brick, limestone and wood to build them, as well as the services of the Bricklayers' Guild, the Stonemasons' Guild and the Carpenters' Guild. You also need peasants from Work Camps to haul the heavy bricks and stones to the work site once enough is stored in the Storage Yards.

Brick-Core Pyramids can be small, medium, large, Pyramid Complex and grand Pyramid Complex.

Sphinxes

The Sphinx is an elaborately carved and painted protector of Pyramids.

To build a Sphinx, you must first find a location. Pick

"Sphinx" from the Religious Structures: Monuments list. A footprint of the sphinx appears. As you move this footprint around the landscape, it will either be green or red. When the footprint is green, then you have found a suitable hidden deposit of stone. Click the mouse button, and the stone will be revealed.

Now, the stonemasons and carpenters can get to work, assuming that you have the necessary wood. Carpenters build scaffolding that stonemasons climb to carve the Sphinx.

Info-click on the Sphinx to visit the Construction

Foreman for a progress report.

Obelisks

Obelisks symbolize the rays of the sun, and great deeds and achievements are commemorated on the sides of the monument.

Obelisks are made from a large amount of granite, and all the granite needed for the Obelisk must be stored in the city's Storage Yards before you can place the monument.

Move the cursor over the land to pick a location for the Obelisk. If you see a green footprint of the monument, you can place the obelisk.

After you pick a location for the Obelisk, the granite is put into place. Then, carpenters from the Carpenters' Guild build scaffolding around the monument, and stonemasons come to the monument to carve intricate designs into it. You do not need the services of peasants to build an Obelisk.

Info-click on the monument to visit the Construction Foreman. He will update you on the status of the monument.

Sun Temples

Sun Temples pay special honor to the Sun Cult that most pharaohs hold very dear.

To build a Sun Temple, you will need sandstone and wood, plus the services of the

Carpenters' Guild, Stonemasons' Guild and Work Camp.

Sun Temples start with a sandstone obelisk. Before the obelisk can be built, adequate supplies of sandstone must be stored in the city's Storage Yards. Once there is enough sandstone, the Sun Temple can be placed. Choose Sun Temple from the Religious Structures: Monuments list, and choose a location. If you have chosen a good location, you will see a green footprint of the monument. After you have chosen a good location, construction of the sandstone obelisk within the Sun Temple begins.

After the stone is placed, carpenters build scaffolding around the obelisk. Then, stonemasons decorate the sides of the sandstone obelisk. When they have finished the obelisk, they begin work on the remainder of the Sun Temple. First, they build a Vestibule and then a stone Wall. After the Wall is complete, the stone-

masons build the Fore Temple. To complete these elements, stonemasons need several sledge loads of sandstone delivered by peasants. While they are working on the Fore Temple, Wall and Vestibule, stonemasons install decorative tiles between the Walls.

Once the Fore Temple is complete and all the tiles have been laid, the Sun Temple is finished.

Mausoleums

Mausoleums are large tombs used to inter pharaohs and nobility.

To build a Mausoleum, supplies of sandstone and wood are needed, plus at least one working Carpenters' Guild, Stonemasons' Guild and Work Camp.

To place a Mausoleum, there must first be a large quantity of sandstone stored in the city's Storage Yards. Once enough stone is stored, choose Mausoleum from the Religions Structures: Monuments list. Place the Mausoleum, using the color of the footprint as a guide (green means you can place the structure, red means you cannot). Once you've designated a place for the building, peasants from the Work Camp clear the land and lay the foundation.

Once the foundation is in place, stonemasons begin work. Whenever a Storage Yard accumulates four blocks of sandstone, peasants load the stone on a sledge and drag it to the construction site. Stonemasons put the stone in place until the first story is completed. Then, carpenters install wooden ramps so that the stonemasons can work on the second story of the Mausoleum. When the second story is complete, the Mausoleum is finished.

Burial Provisions

To ensure that the deceased has all he or she needs in the afterlife, you must stock most tombs with burial provisions. Burial provisions are materials that the deceased used while alive. You may also need to provide materials for the construction of special accouterments needed for the afterlife, such as a funeral barge and sarcophagus. Monuments are not complete until you have supplied any required burial provisions. The Overseer of Monuments has a list of the necessary

items and the desired quantities. When you are ready to send them, tell the Overseer of Monuments to dispatch goods to the tomb.

You do not have to have the full amount of the required material in the Storage Yards before you can send goods to the monument. You can send smaller portions of the required commodity until you have fulfilled the requirement.

Your city may need to import some burial provisions.

Monument Building Tips

Monuments take years to build, but there are a few things you can do to expedite the process.

Build plenty of the required Guilds and Work Camps. The more Guilds and Work Camps you have, the quicker the monument can be built.

Build specialized Storage Yards near the monument site. Make sure you have plenty of Storage Yards around the construction site, and give these Storage Yards special orders to ensure that they carry only the materials needed to construct the monument. Having Storage Yards near the construction site cuts down on peasants' travel time as they drag sledges full of building materials to the site.

Make sure you are obtaining enough construction materials. Some monuments require a massive amount of stone or brick. Make sure you have enough quarries or Brickworks working in your city to keep a high volume available. If your city is unable to quarry its own stone or make its own bricks, make sure you are importing as much stone or bricks as you can.

While monuments are made of stone and/or brick, most also require a supply of wood. Remember that carpenters need to build ramps or scaffolding for many of your monuments. Make sure you have a Carpenters' Guild working in the city, and make sure that the guild has a supply of wood.

Also, build the Carpenters' Guild as close to the monument site as possible, even if this means that the guild will be far away from the nearest supply of wood. The carpenters will have plenty of time to stock up on wood while the bricklayers and stonemasons are busy at their tasks. But, when the stonemasons and bricklayers need a ramp, all work stops until the carpenter makes his way to the monument site to build the ramp. The longer his trip, the longer construction will stall.

Visit the Construction Foreman for a monument status report. The Construction Foreman knows how much progress has been made on the monument and what might be holding up work.

Remember to dispatch any necessary burial provisions. Some monuments are not complete until you have stocked them with the required burial provisions. Visit your Overseer of Monuments to find out which items are needed and to send them to the monument.

Health

While Egyptians look forward to entering the Field of Reeds after death, they're not particularly keen on cutting their lives on earth short. The Egyptians consult physicians to maintain their general health. The rely on herbalists for medicines and insect repellent, while dentists help them combat tooth decay. And, when the time finally comes to face Osiris and to have their souls weighed against Ma'at's feather, embalmers ensure that the deceased are ready for the journey.

Health Buildings

Several professionals in the city concern themselves with citizens' health. Many illnesses can strike the city's inhabitants, and providing them with access to health professionals helps to mitigate their chances of taking ill. Each professional has his own building, and you will see them listed when you click the Health and Sanitation Structures button on the Control Panel.

Health and Sanitation Structures Button

> **Water Supply.** Water carriers from Water Supplies bring clean drinking water to the city's residents. Clean drinking water helps reduce the likelihood of a malaria outbreak.

Water Supply

> **Physician's office.** Physicians from Physician's offices walk through neighborhoods, taking care of people's general health.

Physician's office

> **Apothecary.** Herbalists from Apothecaries distribute insect repellent made from animal fat to the city's neighborhoods. The use of insect repellent helps reduce the risk of malaria.

Apothecary

Mortuary

Dentist's office

Mortuaries. At Mortuaries, embalmers prepare the dead for their final journey to the afterlife. Properly preparing the dead promotes a city's overall health which helps prevent plague. To wrap the deceased's body, embalmers use linen made by a weaver or imported from a trade partner.

Dentists. Sand is everywhere in Egypt, even in food, and continuously crunching on sand quickly wears down teeth. Wealthier citizens want to take care of their teeth, and turn to dentists to keep their smiles bright. Dentists do not impact city health, but they do improve a neighborhood's desirability.

All the above health structures require both road access and labor to operate.

City Health and Health Risks

The health of each resident in the city contributes to overall City Health. Generally, to remain healthy, each resident needs plenty of food and frequent visits from a physician. A varied diet and access to a Mortuary supplement a resident's health.

Three health threats stalk the city: disease, malaria and plague. Providing good healthcare to each citizen is the key to preventing disease and plague from striking. Malaria, on the other hand, only threatens certain areas of the city, particularly those along the water and near marshland. To protect citizens who live in these areas from succumbing to this deadly ailment, make sure to provide them with clean drinking water and the insect repellents provided by herbalists.

Each of the health threats behaves in a different way:

Disease

Disease occurs in homes that do not have good access to a physician and a steady supply of food. Disease

Plagued Citizen

The Herbalist's Craft
Shomu, 13th year of Ramesses
Morning
Dear Journal

Khmunhotep and I set out early this morning. The agenda: fishing on the Nile. But first, we stopped at the Apothecary to outfit ourselves with some basic necessities.

The herbalist greeted Khmunhotep, and they began talking of a recent malaria outbreak. The herbalist said he did all that he could, but that once malaria breaks out it's hard to stop.

While they talked, I selected my items for purchase. First, some I bought some kohl to put around my eyes. Kohl helps to reduce the sun's glare which can be almost blinding. Then, I purchased some insect repellent made from hippo's fat. While the unguent had a noxious smell, it was well worth it. Mosquitoes are always a nuisance on the Nile, and their bites sting. Well stocked with supplies, we head for the Nile.

We borrowed a fishing raft made from reeds and set out. We caught a lot of fish, even the sacred oxyrhynchus fish which we threw back.

By midmorning, we had our fill of fishing and returned to the shore.

strikes individual domiciles and does not spread. If an entire neighborhood has poor access to physicians, however, disease can break out in more than one home. When disease strikes, there is nothing to be done for the afflicted. Everyone living in the home dies.

Use the Risks: Disease overlay (page 205) to see which homes are most likely to become diseased. Build more Physician's offices in the area to reduce the risk. You can also use the Health: Physician overlay (page 207) to help you plan the placement of Physician's offices. The Physician overlay shows you the access each home has to a physician, as well as the physician himself making his rounds.

Malaria

Living among marshes and along the water means living with the risk of malaria. Homes on grassland close to the river and to reed-filled marshes are most at risk. The denser the grass, the higher the risk of malaria.

Like disease, malaria begins in a single house. Unlike disease, though, malaria soon spreads through the air to neighboring homes. The only way to reduce the chance of a malaria outbreak is by having plenty of Water Supplies and Apothecaries in the areas of the city which are most susceptible. Use the Risks: Malaria overlay (page 205) to see which homes are particularly at risk for malaria.

If one person living in a house has malaria, all the house's residents die.

Plague

If overall health conditions are particularly bad in the city, plague can break out. The only way to prevent plague is to ensure that your city provides for *all* your citizens' health needs — especially plentiful diets and access to physicians.

Plague is an insidious ailment, and there is no way of predicting where it will first break out. Plague is strictly the result of poor overall city health; it is not related to an individual home's risk of malaria or disease.

Once a home is plagued, one of the poor, sickened residents emerges from the house, fevered and distraught, and begins wandering the city's streets. Every house he passes becomes infected, no matter how good that house's access to healthcare is or how wealthy its occupants are. All the residents of the homes the plagued walker passes perish. To prevent this catastrophe, be sure to provide the necessary healthcare to everyone in your city.

Plagued walkers journey around your city because they know that their situation is dire. Should an herbalist encounter a plagued citizen, he is under strict orders to remove that person from the city's streets in whatever way he can. A plagued person will die after one month if he never encounters an herbalist.

Herbalists can help to contain plague once it arises, but only good city health can prevent outbreaks altogether.

Infected Housing

Once a house has become infected by any illness, it

becomes uninhabitable for a few months. These structures will be marked with a skull. When the house is livable again, the skull icon will disappear and people can move into the housing. The home will not devolve while it's vacant, and whatever supplies it held remain available to its next occupants.

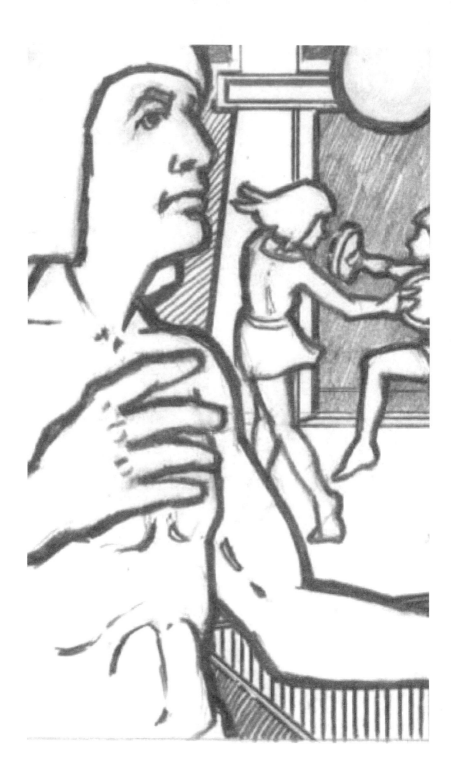

Ah ll work and no play make Amenhotep a dull boy. The Egyptian people enjoy a good spectacle with jugglers, dancers and singers, and like to unwind with a game of senet and a mug of beer at the Senet House.

Providing easy access to entertainment pleases citizens from all walks of life.

Building Entertainment Structures

Build entertainment structures by clicking on the Entertainment Structures button in the Control Panel. All entertainment structures require road access and a staff of workers.

Entertainment
Structures Button

Entertainment Venues

Entertainment venues must be placed on an intersection because they thrive where people meet. They can be tricky to place because of the stages each venue has; use the green "ghost" as a guide. To operate, entertainment venues need labor plus entertainers from performer schools. There are three types of venue, and the largest of them can host a wide variety of entertainers:

Booth. The Booth is the smallest of the entertainment venues. It holds only one stage and only jugglers can perform there. Booths have a positive effect on the surrounding neighborhoods.

Bandstand. Bandstands are medium-sized venues that have two stages: one to host jugglers and the other to to feature performances by musicians.

A Sumptuous Banquet
Shomu, 13th year of Ramesses
Evening

Dear Journal,

What an evening we had this evening! We were invited to a banquet at the local Nomarch's house, and I have never been privy to such a lavish party.

Nefernetka looked resplendent. With the aid of her servant, she spent all day preparing for the evening. She wore a tunic made of the finest linen available and adorned herself with jewels. Her eyes were made up with kohl and galena, and her fingernails dyed with henna. Another servant spent hours grooming the wig that Nefernetka wore.

When we arrived at the party, our host handed each of us a cone of wax to place on our heads and a garland of flowers for our necks. The cone helped to keep our heads cool. We sat down to a sumptuous feast of beef, antelope and fowl accompanied by gorgeous fruits and crisp vegetables. The host had even procured a large supply of wine from distant Mycenae, a rare departure from the usual Egyptian beer. While we ate, a group of musicians began to play, and beautiful dancers leapt about to the music. The revelry continued until all the food had been eaten and all the wine had been drunk.

Enjoying ourselves too much to sleep, Khmunhotep, Nefernetka and I went to the local Senet House where the townspeople gather after work to drink beer and have conversation. Several people were playing games of senet, and a storyteller entertained the crowd with tales of bygone days. We finally went home, but I couldn't sleep. With visions of all that I had seen swirling through my mind, I didn't need to dream.

The juggler's stage is in one corner of the venue, and the band plays on a second stage in another corner. People like to live near Bandstands.

Pavilion. The largest of the entertainment venues, Pavilions have three stages: one for juggling shows, one for musical concerts and one for dance performances. No citizen will complain about living next to a Pavilion.

Training Centers

Citizens expect high-quality entertainment, and training centers make sure that people are entertained by professionals, not amateurs. Each type of performer has his or her own training center: would-be jugglers practice their skills at Jugglers' Schools, musicians attend the Conservatory and dancers hone their craft at Dance Schools.

Jugglers' School

Conservatories and Dance Schools both have a negative effect on a neighborhood's desirability. The cacophony that emits from a Conservatory is not music to residents' ears, and dancers come and go at the strangest hours. People like living near Jugglers' Schools. Jugglers learning their craft engage in some very amusing highjinks.

Senet House

A Senet House offers a place for people to go to enjoy a relaxing game of senet, a contest that depicts the journey to the afterlife. With frothy mugs of beer at their elbows, citizens while away the hours in each other's company and engage in a little friendly competition. In addition to workers and road access, a Senet House needs a supply of beer (see page 76) to serve to its patrons.

People do not like living near Senet Houses. The clientele tends to be loud and boisterous — especially the losers of high-stakes senet games.

Measuring Access to Entertainment

Your Overseer of Diversions keeps track of the number of working jugglers' stages, musicians' stages and dancers' stages in your city, as well as the number of working Senet Houses.

When evaluating their satisfaction with a city's entertainment, the most important thing for citizens is access to as many types of entertainment, or as many different types of stages, as possible. Variety is very important to the city's residents: providing, for example, scores of jugglers to entertain a neighborhood won't go far in satisfying citizens' desire for entertainment. They like being able to choose from various diversions.

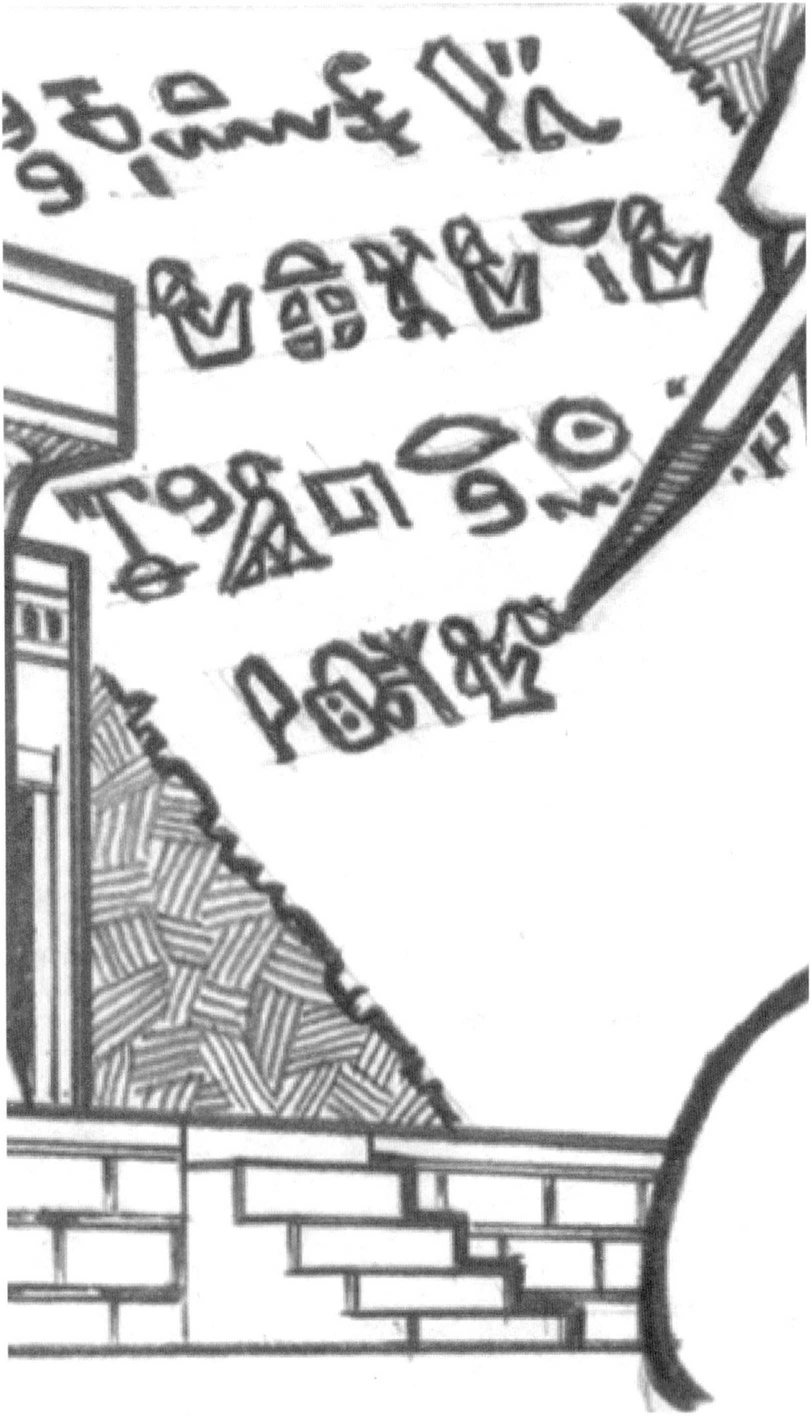

Education

Education is the privilege of the wealthy. The wealthy no longer perform manual labor, and they want their children never to experience the horrors of toiling and sweating under the sun's hot rays. To attain this goal for their children, wealthy scribes like to have Scribal Schools close by. They also like access to Libraries to enhance their own knowledge.

Building Education Structures

Scribal Schools and Libraries are the two types of educational facilities you can build. Construct them by clicking the "Education Structures" button on the Control Panel.

Education Structures
Button

Papyrus

Papyrus, made by papyrus makers from common reeds that grow along the Nile, is a key resource to both Scribal Schools and Libraries. Teachers and librarians use papyrus and cannot bring the benefits of education to your city's wealthier citizens without it. Because they need papyrus to fill their shelves with scrolls, Libraries cannot be built until there is a supply of papyrus stored in the Storage Yards. To keep your education system working, then, it's important to have a thriving papyrus industry or a steady stream of costly papyrus imports.

Scribal Schools

Once a Scribal School is fully staffed and has a stock of papyrus, teachers walk through the city's neighborhoods educating the youth of well-to-do households. Each time a teacher leaves the Scribal School, he takes some papyrus with him so that his pupils can practice

Scribal School

their hieroglyphs. Be sure that you are able to replenish the Scribal School's papyrus supply, or the city's affluent children will not be able to learn their writing.

Libraries

Library

Libraries send librarians through the city's wealthy neighborhoods. The papyrus that is needed to build the library makes up its permanent collection; librarians take additional scrolls of papyrus to circulate works of literature to citizens to read at home. Librarians need additional scrolls of papyrus to maintain the collection, so the Library's supply of papyrus must be replenished if it is to continue to operate.

The Scribe's Art
Shomu, 13th year of Ramesses
Midday

Dear Journal,

Khmunhotep and I entered Per-Ankh, the library where literary, religious, scientific and historical papyri are stored. Most people aren't allowed into the Per-Ankh, but Khmunhotep is a scribe so we were granted entry.

Khmunhotep smiled as he recalled his days as a scholar. 'I was fairly quick in my studies so was liked by the teachers,' he remembered. 'But some of my friends weren't so lucky. My poor friend Nebamun certainly took more than his fair share of beatings. It all worked out for him, though. He works in Pharaoh's palace, keeping track of his household affairs.

Khmunhotep then led me to a room whose walls were lined with holes filled with papyri. Khmunhotep selected one and unrolled it. 'Ah,' he says, 'this is one of my favorites, and it makes me feel good about being a scribe. It's called 'Satire on the Trades,' and it points out the many disadvantages of not being a scribe. When I was first learning how to write, I copied this manuscript over many times.'

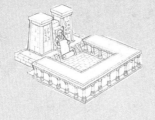

The Military, Combat and Defense

The land seems idyllic with its fertile farms, beautiful temples and luxurious gardens, but all this can quickly change in the face of war. Invasion is a frequent threat, and even battles waged far from the city's borders can have a direct effect on its people. Attack can come from any direction, over land or by water.

You have many means of defending the city from attack. You can build strong Walls to encircle the city, keeping those with foul intentions out. Determined invaders will eventually break through even the strongest Wall, though, so keep a versatile and strong army in your city to prevent disaster.

Some invaders approach your land by sea or river, and no Wall will prevent them from invading. A mighty navy, however, may stop these foes from reaching land.

Military Structures
Button

Raising an Army

In addition to protecting the city from harm, an army can do the city great honor by serving the Kingdom should their assistance be required. To raise an army, build Forts and a Recruiter's office. Military Academies train new men to be better soldiers, but they are not strictly necessary to raise an army.

Recruiter and Academy

When you are ready to raise an army, build a Recruiter's office by clicking the Military Structures

Recruiter

button and choosing Recruiter. Men willing to fight for their city go to the Recruiter's office to enlist. The Recruiter's office needs road access and labor.

The recruiter's function is very simple: he enrolls men into the army and provides them with any special weaponry they might need. To equip would-be infantrymen, the recruiter needs a store of weapons, either imported from a trade partner or made by a Weaponsmith (see page 77). To enlist charioteers, the recruiter needs chariots from a Chariot Maker (see page 77) or from a trade partner. Men who dream of being archers supply their own bows and arrows. The recruiter also assigns enlistees to sentry duty on the city's Walls and in the city's Towers.

Academy

New soldiers leave the Recruiter with dreams of glory and needed weaponry, but with little else. The Academy provides these green soldiers with training in the art of war. To build an Academy, select it from the Military Structures list. An Academy needs road access and labor.

The Academy schools infantrymen, archers and chari-oteers on the finer points of combat. Sentries learn their skills on the job and do not attend the Academy. Once they have completed their studies, the soldiers proceed to their companies.

If there is no Academy in the city, then sol-diers proceed to their companies directly from the Recruiter's office.

Companies and Forts

Each soldier is assigned to a company, and each company has its own Fort. The types of companies and Forts are:

Infantry. Infantrymen are the mainstay of most armies. Specialists in close combat, they fight on the front line of the battle. They move at an average rate of speed. They leave the Recruiter armed with spears as weapons.

Archers. With arrows, archers can attack an enemy from longer range than infantry, but are terrible at close-range battle and won't last long if an enemy engages them directly. They march a little more slowly than infantry. Archers craft their own bows and arrows.

Charioteers. There is nothing more frightening to soldiers than seeing a line of chariots barreling towards them. Chariots are key to breaking the protective formations of your enemies, and once their lines are broken, it will be easier to defeat them. Each charioteer receives a chariot upon leaving the Recruiter.

Soldiers prefer to stay in their Forts when they are not fighting and remain there unless you order them into the field. In their Forts, soldiers can enjoy the camaraderie of their fellow soldiers. Prolonged assignment in the field lowers a company's morale (see page 173).

Forts do not need road access or laborers. They have an extremely negative effect on desirability, so it's best to place Forts on the outskirts of the city.

Company Fighting Ability

When companies are in their Forts, standing in the parade grounds, they look fierce and ready to take on any foe. Not all companies, however, are equally prepared to fight. Both experience and morale affect a company's performance on the battlefield.

Experience. The more experienced a company is, the more effective it will be in combat. A company's overall experience depends on the experience of each of its men.

Soldiers fresh from the Recruiter have no experience and have no idea what to expect in the confusion of battle. Soldiers who endured the rigors of Academy training benefit from their instructors' hard lessons and enter into service with some experience.

All soldiers who survive a battle gain experience from fighting. Each engagement that he walks away from teaches a soldier more about the art of war.

Each soldier impacts a company's overall experience. If a new recruit without Academy training joins a veteran company, he'll bring down its overall experience. Soldiers trained at the Academy will bring down the experience level of your most veteran companies, but might improve the experience level of green companies whose previous members weren't Academy-trained.

Info-click on a company or visit your Overseer of the Military to check on a company's experience.

The red ball on the company's standard provides a rough idea of a company's experience level: the higher the ball is on the flagstaff, the more experience the company has.

Company Morale. A company's morale has a direct impact on the behavior of its soldiers in battle. A company with high morale sticks out the most difficult fight. A company with low morale runs when the fighting becomes too difficult. Companies with very low morale may even refuse to leave their Forts.

A number of factors influence morale. Success in battle, in addition to increasing experience, boosts morale. If a company is outnumbered by its enemy, morale plummets. Morale also sinks if soldiers are kept away from their Forts after a battle. When your city is under no immediate threat, don't march your soldiers around or station them away from their Forts, or their morale might be very low indeed when invaders do appear. Companies prefer sleeping and eating in their Fort to foraging for food in the countryside and sleeping under the stars.

A gold ball on the flagstaff of the company's banner gives you a general indication of the company's morale. Info-click on the company or visit your Overseer of the Military for a more precise report.

Marching Orders

To station a company in the field, or to simply instruct it to move to a new location, click on it and then click on a new location. The company's standard will appear in the new location, and the company will march towards it. To tell a company what to do once they arrive at their new location, either info-click on it or use the a hot key once you've selected a company. You can issue a company the following orders before or after you move them to their new location:

Hold Ground in Tight Formation. In tight formation, soldiers stand as close to each other as possible. Because they have been told to hold ground, they will not leave their position to attack enemies. They will attack any enemy that comes within their range, though.

Tight formation brings the most benefit to infantry. When in tight formation, the infantry

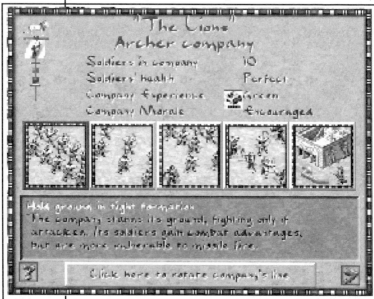

Marching Orders. Click on one of the buttons above to give an order to the selected company. Hold the cursor over an order for a brief description of the command's merits and disadvantages.

form a human wall that can be difficult for enemies to penetrate, and the infantrymen work together to defend each other. They will not move to attack unless attacked first. Archers and charioteers can also line up in tight formation but, because they are not on the front line, the formation does not benefit them as much.

The keyboard command for this order is "T".

Hold Ground in Loose Formation. This command can only be issued to infantry and archers; it cannot be issued to charioteers. In loose formation, your soldiers spread out to cover more ground while holding their positions. They will attack if an enemy comes into range. This formation helps infantry and archers defend themselves against enemy arrows, but does not offer much protection against enemy infantry attack. The keyboard command for this order is "L".

Engage Nearby Enemies. When given this order, a company will move to attack enemies in their immediate vicinity. The attack will continue until the enemy is killed or retreats, or until you issue a different order. The keyboard command for this order is "N".

Mop-Up. When told to mop-up, soldiers seek out any enemies in a wide area and attack them. While under a mop-up order, companies are at their most aggressive, and they fearlessly battle the foe. Fearlessness, however, does hamper their ability to defend themselves, so this order is best used when the city's army outnumbers its enemies. The keyboard command for this order is "M".

Charge. The charge command can be issued only to charioteers. Charging an enemy line breaks up its formation, making the enemy more vulnerable to the attack. When told to charge, the charioteers work the horses up into a lather, and they pull the chariots at top speed for a great distance. Eventually, the horses tire and the chariots slow down and need to rest, so issue this order sparingly. The hot key for this command is "C".

Return to Fort. Click Return to Fort when your soldiers have done their duty and defeated the enemy. At the Fort, they can rest up for the next battle. If morale is low, they'll return to Fort on their own. The hot key for this command is "F".

With most orders, you can decide which direction the soldiers' ranks should run, either this way: /, or that way: \. Click the "Rotate Company" button or press "R" on the keyboard to change the direction the line runs.

In addition to issuing the specific orders outlined above, you can also tell companies to attack by selecting them and clicking on an enemy. The company will pursue the targeted enemy to the death unless you issue a different order.

Weapons, Chariots and their Manufacture

Before infantrymen and charioteers can be assigned to their Forts, the recruiter must outfit them with the implements they will use in battle. The recruiter equips infantrymen with weapons and charioteers with chariots. Weapons are made from copper by a Weaponsmith, and chariots are manufactured using costly wood by Chariot Makers. If the city does not produce these implements of war, it may be able to import them from a trade partner. For more on the manufacture of implements of war, see page 77.

Weaponsmith

Commissioning a Navy

The Nile acts almost as a highway, bringing people, goods and services to the cities along its banks. But, the Nile can also carry invaders who seek to do damage. Building a navy is the best way to prevent these waterborne attackers from reaching land. A navy consists of two types of vessel: the warship and the transport ship.

Building and Berthing Your Ships

Warships and transport ships are constructed by Shipwrights. To start Shipwrights on their task of building mighty war vessels, first make sure the city has an active Shipwright. You can build a Shipwright by clicking on the Industrial Structures button and then choosing Shipwright (see page 77 for more).

Once the Shipwright is active and has a supply of wood, the next step is to build the wharves where the ships will berth. Building wharves and supplying them with workers cues the Shipwright to begin building ships. To build a wharf, select either Warship Wharf or Transport Wharf from the list of buildings you see

Warship Wharf

Transport Wharf

after clicking the Military Structures button. Like all structures built on the shore, wharves must be placed on a straight edge of coast. Ships cannot navigate narrow channels of water, so make sure that the Shipwright's finished boat will have clear sailing to the wharf. Wharves also need road access and a staff of workers. This staff of workers is not the same as the ship's crew, which is drawn from another source and does not reduce the city's population or labor force.

Each wharf berths one ship, warships in Warship Wharves and transport ships in Transport Wharves. When ships are not engaged in battle or transporting troops, it's a good idea to keep them in their wharves.

Warships

Warships patrol the waterways, ramming or shooting at other ships that intend to inflict harm on the city. Warships can also attack land soldiers with missile fire, provided they are near the coast.

Attack Priorities

No matter which order you give a warship, its captain always pursues the same priorities when attacking the enemy. The captain's priorities are:

> **Transport ships with enemy soldiers on board.** The captain knows that his mission has largely failed if enemy soldiers reach land. If there are any transport ships carrying enemy soldiers in the city's waters, he will attack them first.

> **Disembarked enemies near the shore.** The captain's second priority are recently disembarked enemy soldiers. If there are no transport ships

with any enemy soldiers on board stalking the city, he looks for enemies close to shore to punish with a barrage of arrows.

Warships. Enemy warships are his third priority. He will ram enemy warships and try to sink them provided that there are no transport ships with troops aboard or disembarked enemies for your ship to attack.

Empty enemy transport ships. Empty enemy transports are your captain's last priority. He'll attack them if there is nothing else for him to assail.

Your captain reacts quickly to changing situations. He'll abandon a battle if a higher priority situation develops. For example, if he is attacking a warship when a transport ship carrying enemy soldiers sails into the area he is protecting, he'll disengage the enemy warship and target the loaded transport.

Warship Orders

Give a warship orders by info-clicking on it or by selecting it and using a hot key. Warships can carry out the following orders:

Hold Position. When told to Hold Position, the warship will not budge from the spot you designate. It will defend itself by turning face enemy warships to minimize the damage enemies cause by ramming (see page 180) and attack enemies in range by shooting arrows. If several warships are lined up and all have been given the Hold Position order, the warships form a blockade with the goal of keeping invaders out. The keyboard command for this order is "H".

Engage Nearby Enemies. When told to Engage Nearby Enemies, the warship will attack enemies within a small radius of its location. The keyboard command for this order is "N".

Seek and Destroy All Enemies. When given this command, the warship patrols the water looking for enemies to defeat. The keyboard command for this order is "A".

Repair. Should the warship be damaged in a conflict, clicking this button sends the ship to the Shipwright for needed repairs. When the Shipwright is finished fixing the ship, it returns to its home wharf. If the warship is severely damaged, the ship's captain will order it to the Shipwright for repairs on his own. The keyboard command for this order is "R".

Return to Wharf. Clicking on this option sends the ship back to its home wharf. The keyboard command for this order is "W".

To simply tell a warship to move, click on it and then click on a new location. When it arrives at the new spot, it will follow the last order given. If you click on an enemy, the warship will pursue the targeted enemy until it is defeated or, if it is a land target, until it is out of range.

Ramming
Warships attack other ships primarily through ram-

ming. Enemy ships can be rammed at normal speed, but warships moving at top speed inflict the maximum amount of damage. A warship can travel at top speed for only a limited time before its crew, after pulling on the oars for all it is worth, is drained of its strength (see below).

The warship's goal is to inflict as much damage as possible on the enemy ship with one hit. The best place to ram an enemy ship is in its beam, at the center of the side of the ship. Striking the fore quarter inflicts a moderate amount of damage, and a lesser amount of damage is caused by hitting the aft quarter. Ramming the bow of the ship results in slight damage, and a collision with the other ship's stern inflicts hardly any damage at all.

Ship Damage and Hull Strength

A warship can be damaged if it is rammed or hit with missile fire by another ship. Your enemies have the same goal as the city's warships do: to ram ships at their weakest point. Keep a close eye on the status of your ships by info-clicking on them or visiting your Overseer of the Military (see page 187). If you notice that a warship's hull is weak, consider sending it to the Shipwright for repairs. A warship with a weak hull will have difficulty withstanding an enemy attack.

Crew Condition

Warships rely on rowers for maximum propulsion. Rowers are quite strong and can row all day at normal speed. When forced to row at top speed in order to ram, however, their strength will be quickly sapped.
To find out how a warship's crew is feeling, info-click on the warship or visit the Overseer of the Military.

The levels of crew strength are:

Exhausted. Exhaustion sets in after a warship's crew has rowed at top speed for as long as it can. A warship can't move at all while its crew is exhausted — they can't so much as pick up an oar and are completely vulnerable. The only remedy to crew exhaustion is rest, which takes time.

Tired. A tired crew can move its ship, but not very fast. You can give the crew orders, but they can only move their ship at half-speed. Even while rowing at half-speed, though, they will recover from being tired.

Rested. A warship's crew can do anything asked of it when rested.

Transport Ships

Transport ships carry your army across the river or over the sea to far-away lands. Any company can board a transport ship, but a transport ship can carry only one company at a time.

Transport Ship Orders

As with warships, you can give transport ships specific orders. To move a transport ship from one location to another, click on it and then click on a new location. Info-click on the transport ship, or select a transport ship and use the keyboard commands, to issue any of the following commands:

Hold Position. This commands the transport ship to stay where it is. If the transport ship comes under attack, the captain will rotate the ship in an effort to reduce damage. He will not, however, set sail to evade the attack. This option should be used cautiously, because transport ships are not well-equipped to defend themselves. The keyboard command for this order is "H".

Evade Enemies. Transport ships, especially those filled with your soldiers, are both valuable and vulnerable. Click on Evade Enemies to give the transport ship's captain the ability to use all his powers to avoid attack. Evade Enemies is the transport ship's default order, and the ship's captain will pursue this course of action unless you tell him otherwise. The keyboard command for this order is "E".

Embark/Disembark. To load a company of soldiers onto the transport ship, first click the Embark button, then click on the company of soldiers you wish to move over the water. The soldiers will board the transport ship, and the ship will display the company's standard. When you info-click on the transport ship, information on the company on board is displayed.

To return the soldiers to shore, click Disembark, then move the cursor to the location in which you wish to station the company.

The Embark/Disembark option toggles back and forth depending on whether there are soldiers currently on the transport ship. There is no keyboard command for this order

Repair. If the transport ship is damaged, click on repair to send the ship back to the Shipwright for repairs. The ship's captain will bring his ship to the Shipwright on his own if the hull is severely damaged. The hot key for this command is "R".

Return to Wharf. Click on this button to send the transport ship back to its wharf. The hot key for this command is "W".

Hull Strength

Info-click on the transport ship to ascertain its hull's strength and the status of any companies which may be on board. Hull strength is a measure of the ship's seaworthiness. A damaged hull makes the transport ship more vulnerable in the event of an attack.

Defensive Structures

The army and navy defend the city after enemies have penetrated its borders. Building defensive structures may prevent enemies from ever setting foot on the city's soil.

Walls

The most basic defensive structure is the Wall. To build Walls, choose them from the Military Structures: Defensive Structures list. Click and drag the mouse to build large sections of a Wall at one time.

Walls that are a single layer thick only slow down enemies a little. To best defend your city from attack, build Walls several layers thick. It takes enemy soldiers much longer to break through a thick Wall.

Walls are built from ordinary stone, so no stone needs to be quarried or imported to build them.

Towers

Build Towers to bring a little offense to your defensive walls. Towers are manned with guards who are trained by the Recruiter to hurl javelins on any enemies brave or foolhardy enough to come within range.

Provided the Wall is wide enough for them to walk on, Towers also send out sentries to patrol the length of the Wall and rain arrows on approaching enemies.

Towers must be built into Walls that are two layers thick. They also require road access, employees and sentries from a Recruiter's office.

Gatehouses

As comforting as it may seem, you cannot complete-ly encircle your city with Walls. To let immigrants and merchant trade caravans in, you must have Gatehouses.

Gatehouse

Build Gatehouses directly over the major access roads to your city. While you are holding the mouse cursor over the desired location, press "R" to change the direction the Gatehouse is facing. Once placed, Gatehouses will automatically attach to any adjacent Walls. If attack is threatened, guards will close the gates to keep out the enemy.

Like Roadblocks, Gatehouses permit destination walkers free passage but turn roaming walkers back.

Enemies

You will likely encounter several dif-ferent enemies while directing your dynasty to glory. Foreign enemies in *Pharaoh* include:

Nubians
Kushites
Hittites
Hyksos
Libyans
Sea People
Canaanites
Bedouin
Mitanni

Civil wars may erupt during periods of unrest, and sometimes you may find yourself at war with your fellow Egyptians.

The military also helps to protect your city against attack from dangerous, predatory animals. Soldiers and sentries will kill predators when their paths cross. If left to run rampant, predators can decimate a city's population. Keep a watchful eye out for hyenas, crocodiles and hippopotamuses.

Kingdom Service

Sometimes, Pharaoh or the governor of another city may need additional troops to defend a city against attack or to conquer a foreign land. When troops from your city are needed, Pharaoh and other cities are not shy about asking you to send them. To send companies and ships to aid your compatriots, visit your Overseer of the Military and tell him which companies and ships should be made available for Kingdom service and to dispatch them. Your Political Overseer can also send troops and warships to battle once they have been tagged by your Overseer of the Military. If multiple requests for the same type of troop are outstanding, you must visit the Political Overseer to tell him where to dispatch the city's soldiers.

Overseer of the Military

The Overseer of the Military keeps track of the army and the navy. Switch between the army and navy status reports by clicking on the button in the lower right corner.

The army status report displays each company's name, the number of soldiers in each company and its experience level. You can visit any company by clicking the "Go to Company" button. You can also issue a command for a company to return to its fort or to make it available for Kingdom service and to dispatch them.

At the bottom of the screen is an update of military activity in Egypt. If any enemies are approaching the city by land or if Pharaoh or another city has requested your army's aid, it is reported here.

The navy status report provides similar information. It

lists all warships and tells the current condition of the crew and the ship's hull. Click on the "Go to Ship" button to visit a specific warship. You can also earmark a warship for Kingdom service from the navy report and command a ship to return to its wharf. The report also lists how many transport ships you have in the city.

The navy status report also tells of any enemies are approaching by water, and if anyone has asked for the navy's aid.

World Map

If an enemy army or navy is approaching, you will see it on the World Map. Tracking its progress can help you plan your defenses. Similarly, if you have sent any companies or ships to the aid of another city or Pharaoh, you can trace their movements on the World Map.

I t's not enough to build a city, you must build a city well. Ratings are a measure of how good a city is, and all cities are rated in four areas: Culture, Prosperity, Monuments built and Kingdom service.

Building monuments is usually the biggest challenge, but sometimes your city must also attain certain ratings to win a mission. These goals are specified in mission briefings.

Ratings Overseer

Your Ratings Overseer (see page 199) keeps track of the city's current ratings and provides advice on how to improve them. Visit him often to see how your city is doing.

Your Ratings Overseer uses both numbers and columns to display ratings. The numbers are the city's actual ratings, and the columns show how far along you are to meeting the goals set out for your city in the Mission Briefing. If the column is capped, then you have met this goal.

Culture Rating

The Culture Rating measures how many entertainment, education, health and religion buildings your city has against how many citizens live in the city. The more citizens your city has, the more of each kind of structure your city will need to maintain a high Culture Rating.

The best way to boost a city's Culture Rating is to make sure it has more than enough entertainment,

The Apothecary does not affect the city's Culture Rating. The Physician's office, Mortuary and Dentist's office do increase a city's Culture Rating.

education, health and religion buildings to meet the needs of its citizens. Check with your Overseers of Diversion, Learning, Temples and Public Health to see if the city is lacking in any of these services.

Prosperity Rating

The Prosperity Rating is a measure of a city's wealth and its financial security. The rating goes far beyond an assessment of the city's treasury: it also looks at the wealth of its citizens, taking into account property value, unemployment and types of food eaten. To keep a city's Prosperity Rating rising, try to accomplish the following:

Keep the city solvent. Debt generally has a negative impact on a city's Prosperity Rating. If, however, the city is in debt due to construction costs, its Prosperity Rating won't be affected. Money spent on construction is not really lost, it is invested in the city.

Export more than the city imports. If the city's trade balance is positive (it earns more in exports than it spends on imports), your city's Prosperity Rating will receive a boost. A trade deficit reduces its rating.

Make sure the city can pay tribute every year. Missed tribute payments not only damage your relationships with others in the Kingdom (see Kingdom Rating), they also hurt a city's Prosperity Rating. Make sure the city has enough money in its coffers at the end of the year when it is time to pay the Kingdom its due. Consider donating some of your family savings (see page

108) if it will help get the tribute paid.

Keep citizens employed and the city's jobs filled. Both unemployment and labor shortages will damage the Prosperity Rating. A city's Prosperity Rating benefits most if you keep the unemployment rate down to between zero and five percent.

Pay workers high wages. If the city pays more in wages than what others in the Kingdom pay, its Prosperity Rating will benefit. Paying below what the Kingdom pays will cost the city some Prosperity Rating points.

Feed people a variety of foods. The more types of food you provide your citizens, the better the chances for a high Prosperity Rating.

Take steps to improve the city's housing stock. Low-quality housing severely limits a city's Prosperity Rating. No matter how well the city provides food and jobs for its citizens, if it does not provide attractive housing, the Prosperity Rating will not climb.

Encourage workers to become scribes. Having a good percentage of scribes in your population provides a boost to your Prosperity Rating. Remember, though, that scribes do not work, so the city will need to attract more immigrants to take the scribes' places in the work force.

In addition to the above, a Temple Complex, Senet House and a completed monument adds to a city's Prosperity Rating.

If you have trouble raising the city's Prosperity, look for the opposites to the positive influences listed above. Chronic debt, trade deficits, missed tribute, employment troubles, low wages, poor diet and low-level housing all drag Prosperity down.

Kingdom Rating

The Kingdom Rating assesses your relationship with others in Egypt. The best way to keep this rating high is to devote yourself to serving the Kingdom. Respond to requests for goods or military aid whenever you can, and do not cave into requests from the Kingdom's enemies.

Make sure the city pays tribute every year by ensuring that there is money in the coffers at the end of the year. The amount of tribute the city owes is based on the size of its population and whether it earned a profit during the year. You can learn your current tribute level by visiting your Overseer of the Treasury.

Take care not to go into debt. Going into debt will also lower your Kingdom Rating. Others in the Kingdom will begin to think that you are taking advantage of the Kingdom's generosity and frown upon you.

You can also boost your Kingdom Rating by distributing your wealth to the Kingdom by sending gifts from your family savings (see page 108).

Monument Rating

The Monument Rating assesses both the size and scope of any monuments in the city, as well as how far along they are in construction. If you complete all the monuments required and remember to dispatch any necessary burial provisions to provide for the deceased's afterlife, you will have no problem meeting the Monument Rating goal.

There is much to keep track of as you govern a city: farms, industry, the health and well-being of its citizenry, your standing with the Kingdom — the list is almost endless. Luckily, you have a myriad of information sources at your disposal to help you make wise decisions.

Your Overseers

Your Overseers have the most accurate, up-to-date information about the city. Visit them frequently to keep track of all the goings-on in the city. In addition to providing information, your Overseers help you manage the city.

Overseer of the Workers

The Overseer of the Workers reports employment figures in each employment sector. He tells you how many unemployed workers there are in your city. In the case of labor shortages, he shows by how many workers each employment sector is short.

In the event of a labor shortage, you can use your Overseer of the Workers to set labor allocation priorities. Without set priorities, the Overseers of the Workers fills posts as he sees fit, generally favoring the food production sector. If you would like him to make another sector his top employment priority, click on the sector in the list. A screen pops up with a list of numbers, one through nine. Assign a priority level by clicking one of the numbers. Your Overseer of the Workers then funnels workers to sectors in the order that you have set them. If you change one of your priorities, the other prioritized sectors will readjust accordingly.

The Overseer of the Workers also tracks the city's current annual wage level per ten workers and the level that other cities in the Kingdom pay their workers.

Overseer of the Military

The Overseer of the Military keeps track of both branches of the armed forces. The Overseer's army status report updates you on the number and types of companies in the army. He keeps tabs on their morale and experience level and can also send them for Kingdom service should Pharaoh or another city require their aid.

HIs navy status report tells you everything you need to know about the navy's warships and transport ships. He reports each warship crew's fatigue level and the hull's strength. He can also send warships to aid Pharaoh or another city, if needed.

The Overseer also knows if invaders are approaching and if anyone is requesting military aid.

Political Overseer

Your Political Overseer helps you maintain good relations with others in Egypt. He keeps track of all outstanding requests for goods and food and lets you know when there is enough in the Storage Yards to comply with the request. When you are ready to send the required goods or food, the Political Overseer helps make sure the items are dispatched in a speedy manner.

The Political Overseer also keeps track of your family savings and your personal salary. Visit him if you want to adjust your salary level or spend a portion of your family savings (see page 108 for more on both of these topics).

Ratings Overseer

The Ratings Overseer charts current ratings levels and provides advice on how to improve the city's ratings. Click on each rating for advice on how to improve the city's performance. See pages 190-195 for more on ratings in *Pharaoh*.

Overseer of Commerce

Your Overseer of Commerce monitors the city's industries and Storage Yards and keeps track of supply, demand and prices for goods throughout the world. He knows how much of each commodity is stored in the city and tells you whether an item can be imported or exported.

Your Overseer of Commerce also updates you on the current status of each industry. Visit him to turn city industries on or off (see page 55 for more) or to stockpile a particular good in the city's Storage Yards. When a good is being stockpiled, it accumulates quickly in the Storage Yards because no one can use it. It cannot be traded, and Bazaar buyers cannot procure the good for their customers. If a raw material is being stockpiled, no shipments of the commodity will be delivered to its corresponding manufacturer.

To shut down an industry or stockpile a commodity, click on an item in the Overseer of Commerce's list. Buttons with your different options appear in the panel that pops up.

Your Overseer of Commerce also helps you establish

the flow of trade. He identifies which commodities can be imported or exported. Once you have agreed to trade an item, visit him and specify which items to trade by clicking on them. You can tell him how much should be kept in the city's Storage Yards, or you can rely on his judgement and allow him to import and export food and goods as he sees fit. When importing, your Overseer will continue to import a good as long as the city has less than the chosen level. When exporting, your Overseer will export goods any time the city has more then the chosen level.

See pages 91-95 for more on trade.

Overseer of the Granaries

Your Overseer of the Granaries provides information about the city's population and its eating habits. The Overseer offers three different population charts: population history, population by age and population by dwelling. Population-History shows how the city's population size has changed over time. Population-Census shows the city's population by age. Population-Society breaks population down by type of dwelling.

Your Granaries Overseer also discusses anticipated population trends based on the current levels of immigration or emigration. He tells you if the city is producing enough food to feed its citizens and how much food is stored in the Granaries. He also reports the number of immigrants that arrived during the previous month and knows how many people the city's vacant housing can hold.

Overseer of Public Health

Your Overseer of Public Health reports on the city's overall health. He tracks the number of Physician's offices, Dentist's offices, Apothecaries and Mortuaries working in the city and knows if any particular health problems face the city. He also keeps you up-to-date on citizens' latest healthcare demands.

Having more than enough of Physician's offices, Dentist's offices and Mortuaries in a city also increases its Culture Rating (see page 191). Check in with your Overseer of Public Health frequently to make sure the city has enough health care buildings. Because not every city needs them, the Apothecary has no effect on the city's Culture Rating.

Overseer of Learning

Your Overseer of Learning apprises you of the status of education in the city. He reports the number of active Scribal Schools and Libraries and how many people can benefit from existing education structures. He assess-

es the adequacy of access to education and also reports any demands your citizens are making for new education structures. Meeting citizens' demands for education can also boost the city's Culture Rating.

Overseer of Diversions

Your Overseer of Diversions knows how many juggler's stages, musicians' stages and dancers' stages are working in the city. He also reports the number of Senet Houses that are entertaining the public. He estimates how many people can benefit from your city's stages and gauges citizens' satisfaction with their entertainment options. He can also help you improve the city's Culture Rating. If he reports that access to entertainment is inadequate, build more entertainment structures to boost the rating.

Overseer of the Temples

Your Overseer of the Temples knows which gods are worshiped in the city and whether or not the city has a patron god. He also assesses how appeased the gods are. He reports how many Shrines, Temples and Temple Complexes are working in the city and if people are demanding more access to religious facilities. He can also help plan a festival (see page 124 for more). Ensuring that citizens have good access to religion improves the city's Culture Rating.

Overseer of the Treasury

Your Overseer of the Treasury keeps a ledger of the city's income and expenditures. He provides the previous year's ledger for purpose of comparison. Go to your Overseer of the Treasury to set a new tax rate and to see what percentage of the population is currently registered to pay taxes. He also tells how much more money the city would make if everyone was registered for the tax.

Chief Overseer

The Chief Overseer, a sort of Overseer of the Overseers, is the most important Overseer in the city. Your Chief Overseer works with your other Overseers to provide a summary of the city's status in a number of areas. He alerts you to pressing problems that should be dealt with immediately. He's a good person to turn to if you're not sure what problems face the city. He can help you decide what to do to make your city a better place to live.

Your Chief Overseer also knows the latest Nilometer prediction regarding the coming flood and when it is anticipated to occur. He is also the source for information regarding City Sentiment. If citizens are not happy, your Chief Overseer will let you know so, and why.

Overseer of Monuments

Your Overseer of Monuments provides a list of monuments that are required to win a mission and a general status report on any monument construction projects. He also oversees the dispatch of burial provisions for tombs should they be required.

Overlays

If you want to learn more about a certain aspect of the city, viewing the city with an overlay could give you the information you need. Overlays can be essential as you plan a city.

For more specific information on any monument, info-click on the monument site to check in with the Construction Foreman (see page 131).

Water Overlay

With the Water Overlay activated, you can see all your city's Water Supplies and Wells and watch water carriers conduct their daily business.

The Water Overlay is color-coded to give you information on water access in the city. Light blue indicates the presence of ground water. You can place buildings that need access to ground water, like Wells, Water Supplies, Palaces and Mansions, there. Land marked with dark blue shows the houses that have access to water from a Well. Access to clean water from water carriers is marked with blue columns. The taller the column, the better house's access to clean water is.

Risks Overlays

Many potential problems threaten a city's well-being, but luckily you can do something about most of them. The Risks Overlays are your guides to these problems and can help you decide what to do to prevent problems.

In each of the Risks Overlays, most of the buildings will be flattened and replaced with a red column. The taller and redder the column, the greater the risk is.

> **Fire**. The Fire Overlay shows which buildings have a high likelihood of catching fire. You will also be able to see at a glance where the city's Firehouses are, which will help you decide if a particular area may need more protection.

> **Crime**. In any city, some neighborhoods are rougher than others. The Crime Overlay shows you where trouble spots are and where things are

peaceful. The Crime Overlay also shows you the location of Police Stations and Courthouses.

Disease. The specter of disease can haunt your city at every turn. The Disease Overlay shows you where pestilence thrives. It also shows the physicians in your city who combat this risk.

To see where your health workers are, use the Health Overlay (see page 207).

Malaria. Malaria-carrying mosquitoes live in marshes and near water. Homes in these locations are susceptible to malaria infection. Using the Malaria Overlay shows you which homes are most at risk and shows you the herbalists working in the city to prevent the affliction.

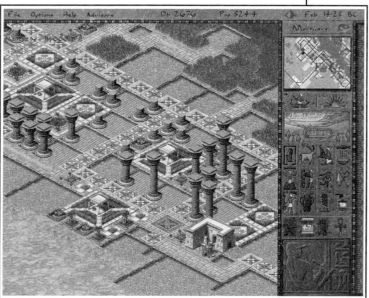

Overlays. Overlays show you particular aspects of your city. This overlay shows which homes have access to a Mortuary. The homes have been flattened and replaced with columns. The higher the column, the better access the house has to a Mortuary.

Damage. While building techniques are quite advanced, some structures in the city are prone to collapse and failure. The Damage Overlay shows you which structures are most likely to fall down. The Damage Overlay also shows the architects patrolling the city.

Problems Overlay

Any of a number of problems can strike the city, and it can be difficult to tell when a problem is about to happen. With the Problems Overlay, you can identify at-risk buildings before problems occur.

When the Problems Overlay is enabled, all the buildings in your city that are not working correctly are displayed. On the lower part of each building are icons that indicate any problems it is suffering. If you hold the mouse cursor over an inactive building, balloon help describes the problem.

For all buildings in the city, the Problems Overlay shows which are about to collapse or catch fire. For housing and industrial buildings, the Problems Overlay uncovers these potential threats:

Housing
About to devolve
About to produce a criminal
About to catch malaria
About to become diseased
Infected
Vacant

Industry
No labor

Partial labor
Shut Down
Needs raw materials

The Problems Overlay also shows any delivery men who are unable to deliver their load of supplies. It also shows representatives from the city's employment sectors who are looking for able-bodied workers. If a building in the city is chronically without labor, keep an eye on its representative to find out why.

Entertainment Overlay

All citizens demand diversion, and some insist on more than one type. The Entertainment Overlay shows housing's access to each type of entertainer and to entertainment overall. Columns on each dwelling show how much access it has to entertainment. The taller the column, the better the access.

The Overall Entertainment Overlay shows aggregate access to all entertainment types.

Education Overlay

For a city to truly thrive, its wealthy citizens must be well educated. The Education Overlay shows which houses have good access to Scribal Schools and Libraries. As with the Entertainment Overlay, you can view the effects of the city's educators in aggregate or by type.

Health Overlays

The Health Overlays show by type how frequently the city's housing is visited by health workers. Keep an eye on your city's dentists, physicians, embalmers and herbalists as they go about their duties.

Administration Overlay

The Administration Overlay covers a range of services that affect the way a city is run.

Tax Income Overlay. Which scofflaws are evading your tax collectors? The Tax Overlay shows who's paying his fair share and who is getting off scot free. The higher the columns, the more frequently a tax collector passes. The stack of coins next to the columns indicates how much tax the house has paid. If you hold the mouse cursor over the coins, mouse help displays the exact amount of tax collected at the property. Based on what you learn, you may decide to build more Tax Collector's offices in the areas that are getting off easy.

Keep in mind, though, that frequent visits by a tax collector does not mean that a house pays more taxes. Taxes are collected only when they are due In order for a house to pay taxes each month, it must have been recently passed by a tax collector.

Desirability Overlay.   The Desirability Overlay indicates where the city's best neighborhoods are. Land is marked with colored squares ranging from brown to gold. The darkest brown squares are the least desirable places to live. Gold squares mark the most desirable locations.

Bazaar Access Overlay. The Bazaar Access Overlay shows which homes are being visited by a seller from the Bazaar. It also shows where the city's Bazaars, Granaries and Storage Yards are.

Security Overlay. This overlay shows all the means

the city has on hand of defending itself. It shows Police Stations, Forts, defensive structures, Warship Wharves, Transport Wharves, Recruiter and Academy. If you have built a Temple Complex to Seth and added the Oracle of Sekhmet (see page 123), you will also see priests of Seth walking your city's streets.

View

As you look out over the city, you start out facing north. If you want to look in a different direction, click on the pyramid icon located at the top of the screen next to the date. If you click on the right side of the pyramid, your view of the city will rotate counter-clockwise 90 degrees. Clicking on the left side of the pyramid will rotate your view 90 degrees clockwise. Clicking on the center of the pyramid will reorient your view due north.

Rotate Map

Viewing the city from a different perspective can be helpful, especially if you are trying to see behind a large structure.

Overview Map

The Overview Map displays a large portion of the city at one time. Buildings are color-coded according to their function as follows:

Roads	Grey
Food and Farming	Bright green
Industry	Red
Entertainment	Light blue
Religion	Dark purple
Education	Yellow
Health	White

Safety and Maintenance	Blue
Government	Lavender
Military	Orange
Beautification	Teal
Monuments	Dark grey
Walls and Gatehouses	Black

A yellow rectangle on the overview map marks the area currently in view. Click on any area of the Overview Map to jump to a new location.

World Map

World Map Button

The World Map shows your city along with other important cities in the world. Open trade routes are clearly marked on the map, and you can chart the progress of enemy armies or navies moving toward the city here. Similarly, if you have sent your own army or navy in aid of another city or of Pharaoh, you can track their movements on the World Map.

Citizens

Citizens in *Pharaoh* are busy taking care of their day-to-day tasks. But, if you check in with them by info-clicking on any of them, they will tell you what they are doing or what they are thinking about. And, the longer you engage them in conversation, the more they will tell you.

Citizens tell you about the most pressing situation as they see it. Not all citizens have the same opinion, though. Still, if hunger is the biggest problem in the city, more citizens will complain about being hungry than anything else.

If you ask citizens to tell you more, they will tell you everything they think about the city, in order of importance.

Citizens, however, do have a slight tendency to exaggerate. While they will give you an idea of the attitude prevailing in the city, your Overseers are a much more reliable source of information. Citizens' opinions tend to be self-centered

Messages

Message Button

When a notable event occurs in the city or elsewhere in the Kingdom, you will receive a message describing the event. Some of these messages are urgent and require quick response on your part. They could be requests from Pharaoh or other cities, or could be directing your attention to a particular trouble spot in your city.

When a new message arrives, the "Message" button on the Control Panel will light up. Click on the button, and your message will be displayed. If the matter is extremely urgent, the message will be delivered to you directly and appear on the screen automatically. If the message is alerting you to some trouble in your city, you can click on the alarm button within the message to proceed directly to the trouble spot.

Other messages you will receive contain instructions that will help you manage the city more successfully. These messages are useful guides that teach important game concepts and set up short-term goals. Meeting the short-term goals outlined in these special messages enables you to win a mission and move on to the next step. These messages are marked with a blue scroll in the message list.

To erase a message, info-click on its title in the message list.

A New Egypt Thrives

As generations have done for countless years, you stand on the edge of the desert, looking out towards the place you call home. The city spreads before you: towards its center, majestic Temples honor the gods, and diplomats and common citizens alike mill around the city's stately Palace. Away from the center are fine neighborhoods decorated with Gardens, Plazas and Statues. On the outskirts of the city are industries and farms that produce goods and foods that the citizenry needs. Caravans make their way to the busy Storage Yards to sell exotic goods from far off lands. The Nile serves as a backdrop to the scene and hosts mighty warships and humble ferry boats.

Turning your back to the city, you face a growing Pyramid that, when the time comes, will house your body as you make your journey to the Field of Reeds. On the walls of the Pyramid, artists are painting your family's story, a story that began centuries ago. All the toiling of your ancestors has led to this moment: a united Egypt, with cities unparalleled in all the world. How difficult it must have been for your earliest forebears to dedicate themselves to Egypt's glory when that glory must have seemed so far away.

As you prepare yourself for your final journey, you can be sure that all who went on before you are proud of your final achievement. Yet, you also know that without the efforts of each of your ancestors, Egypt would not be what it is today. Great Pyramids are made up of individual stones, and great nations are made up of individuals dedicated to a common goal. And, just as the Pyramid needs each stone to be complete, each individual's contributions made it possible for Egypt to be the great land it has become.

Designer's Notes

As we approach the new millennium, somehow the spectacular though enigmatic civilization of ancient Egypt seems to have taken on a new significance for the modern world. Always shrouded by a certain mystique and romanticism, this remarkable culture now seems to reach out at us, evoking familiar but still tantalizing questions about our place in the universe, where we've come from and where we're going. Why does this long dead civilization have such an effect on us?

Could it be simply that the tremendous antiquity of this culture almost defies belief? Indeed, this civilization is so old that the great pyramids were ancient history by the time the Roman Empire arrived on the scene. Maybe it's just that there's a certain kind of magic that we, as human beings, find ourselves believing in, precisely because so much remains unknown about this amazing culture, whose great and wondrous achievements we still marvel at to this day. Though Egypt has certainly endured the test of time, the truth is that on the eve of this new millennium, as we ponder such enticing questions as "is there life on other planets?", there is still quite a lot about the history of our own world we don't know, and may never know.

What we do know about ancient Egypt is fascinating, yet the topic conjures up very different images to just about anyone you ask. To some people, the study of ancient Egypt only means dusty old textbooks and stuffy museums. To others it's the stuff of tabloid headlines, where alien encounters and the resurrection of the dead are an integral part of the picture. Well, with *Pharaoh* we hope we've changed that! In this game, you won't be stuck staring at photographs of crumbling old ruins, or lifeless paintings of long-dead Pharaohs nor will you see flying saucers hovering over the pyramids, or terrifying mummies walking the streets. What you will see in *Pharaoh* is a vivid picture of ancient Egypt brought to life – our version of it anyway.

Just what is our version of life in an ancient Egyptian city? The tremendous challenges of maintaining a huge population, almost exclusively for the purpose of constructing massive monuments of mudbrick and stone, is central to *Pharaoh*, as it was to the rulers of ancient Egypt. Above all else, what made the construction of edifices like the great pyramids and sphinx possible, was the tremendous gift the pharaohs had for organizing and controlling huge numbers of people. This dominant aspect of ancient Egyptian life is a huge part of the *Pharaoh* experience, and something I am sure most strategy gamers can relate to.

In our game, as in ancient Egypt, the successful completion of monuments like the great pyramids (or even a small pyramid for that matter) is a detailed and multi-stepped process. It entails quarrying or importing stone, or making bricks from clay and straw, then using peasants to haul these materials to the construction site where masons and bricklayers (supported by carpenters) set them into place. Block by block the monument rises ever higher and higher - one step at a time. Watching a pyramid or other monument inch its way toward the sky, due to the efforts of an entire population of workers, scribes and peasants, is a real constructive gaming experience, perhaps too often neglected in favor of the destructive, and we hope you'll enjoy this as much as we do.

Another core element of the *Pharaoh* game model is its farming system. Confined to a very narrow ribbon of arable land surrounded by thousands of square miles of barren and inhospitable desert, the ancient Egyptians took advantage of many sources of food, such as wild game, fish and beef cattle — all of which we've included in *Pharaoh*. However, in order for their civilization to truly prosper, Egyptian farmers had to contrive and master some peculiar and innovative farming practices to fully take advantage of the rich and fertile soil (referred to as 'the black land'), which was deposited each year, as the annual inundation of the great Nile river receded. In time almost every facet of Egyptian culture was to some degree bound to this yearly cycle, and for several months of the year (when their fields were entirely covered by water), most peasant farmers contributed to the construction of the great monuments.

For cities located further to the north, in Lower Egypt, the flood waters would come later in the year. If Africa experienced a drought (or if Osiris was displeased), no flood would come. 'Nilometers' were built to help predict the level of the annual flood, and huge granaries were constructed to store the immense annual harvest. Massive irrigation projects were undertaken to extend the benefits of the flood, and, of course, priests always took tremendous pains to ensure that Osiris was appeased.

In *Pharaoh*, to allow you to experience this unique way of life first hand, we've incorporated all of these principles into a detailed, yet simple to use farming system. I could go on and spend hundreds of pages outlining the 'story' behind each facet of *Pharaoh*, but I think the game speaks for itself.

One final note: There is often a tendency to ascribe the success of any really great game (and in case you haven't guessed, we think *Pharaoh* is a really great game) to a single individual "visionary", or "star". Maybe epilogues like these "designer's notes" I'm now writing are evidence of this...I don't know.

I do know, however, that *Pharaoh* could not have been possible without the extraordinary talents of all of the development staff here at Impressions. It has of course been my job (and my pleasure) to lay the foundation for what *Pharaoh* would be, and to provide a (hopefully gentle) guiding hand to keep it on track, but it is the art, programming, production, music, sound design, play testing and writing staff here at Impressions who truly bring a game like *Pharaoh* to life. Each adds his or her own unique touch, while remaining true to the character of what we've collectively created, and once a project like this is underway, it positively takes on a life of its own (which I must say is truly magnificent to see).

What's more, although *Pharaoh* has been largely brought to fruition by a certain "core team" of individuals, in fact by the time any one of our games leaves the studio and enters the world, pretty much everyone at Impressions — including members of other project teams — has contributed something to it. So above all, *Pharaoh* is an Impressions game, and one which I hope will both entertain and inform for years to come.

Chris Beatrice
Cambridge, Massachusetts
September 1, 1999

Appendix 1: Building Summary

Appendix 1: Building Summary

The following chart lists, in alphabetical order, all the buildings you can build in *Pharaoh* except for monuments and housing. Here is a key to the symbols:

Cost. High stacks of coins indicate high construction cost. Low stacks of coins show which buildings put less of a strain on the city's purse strings.

Trash cans mark the buildings that have a negative influence on an area's desirability. The more trash cans you see, the worse the building is for an area's quality.

Flowers denote the buildings that have a positive effect on an area's desirability. Buildings that are most desirable additions to any neighborhood have several flowers marking them.

Some buildings have a risk of catching fire. They are indicated by a flame.

Some buildings are especially prone to collapse and in need of attention from an architect. They are marked by a hammer.

Building	Cost	Employees Needed	Effect on Desirability	Risks	
Academy	(coins)	20	(trash)	(fire) (hammer)	**Military.** Providing Academy training to soldiers increases their experience.
Apothecary	(coin)	5	(flower)	(fire)	Health & Sanitation
Architect's Post	(coin)	5		(hammer)	Municipal
Bandstand	(coins)	12	(flower)	(fire)	**Entertainment.** Has a musicians' stage and a juggler's stage. Must be placed over intersection
Bazaar	(coin)	5	(trash) (trash)	(fire)	**Storage & Distribution.** While it is undesirable to live right next to a Bazaar, it is desirable to live nearby.
Booth	(coins)	8	(flower)	(fire)	**Entertainment.** Has only a juggler's stage. Must be placed over intersection
Brewery	(coins)	12	(trash) (trash) (trash)	(fire)	**Industrial.** Needs a supply of barley to make beer.

Building	Cost	Employees Needed	Effect on Desirability	Risks	
Bricklayers' Guild	🪙	10	🗑️🗑️🗑️	🔥🔨	Industry
Brickworks	🪙	12	🗑️🗑️	🔥	Industry. Makes bricks from straw and clay.
Bridge	🪙	–			Municipal. Cost is per section of bridge; maximum length is four sections.
Carpenters' Guild	🪙	8	🗑️🗑️🗑️	🔥	Industry. Needs a delivery of wood to construct ramps and scaffolding.
Cattle Ranch	🪙	12	🗑️🗑️	🔥	Food & Farming. Needs straw to feed cattle.
Chariot Maker	🪙	30	🗑️🗑️🗑️	🔥	Military. Needs wood to make chariots.
Clay Pit	🪙	8	🗑️	🔨	Industry: Raw Materials.

Building	Cost	Employees Needed	Effect on Desirability	Risks	
Conservatory		8	🗑	🔥	**Entertainment.** Trains musicians to perform on musicians' stages found in Bandstands and Pavilions.
Courthouse		10	✿ ✿	⚒	**Municipal.** Stores a portion of the city's funds.
Dance School		10	🗑	🔥	**Entertainment.** Trains dancers to perform on dancers' stages found only in Pavilions.
Dentist		2	✿	🔥	**Health & Sanitation.** Has no effect on City Health; contributes to to a neighborhood's desirability.
Dock		12	🗑 🗑 🗑 🗑	🔥 ⚒	**Storage and Distribution.** Must be placed on straight edge of coastline in a navigable location.
Farm		10	🗑		**Food & Farming.** Types of farms are Barley, Chickpea, Fig, Flax, Grain, Lettuce and Pomegranate. Only Meadow Farms require employees.
Ferry Landing		5	🗑 🗑		**Municipal.** Ferry Landings must be placed in pairs, one each on opposing sides of the river.

Building	Cost	Employees Needed	Effect on Desirability	Risks	
Festival Square	(coins)	–	(3 flowers)		Religion. Festivals cannot be held without a Festival Square
Firehouse	(coin)	6	(trash)	(fire)	Municipal
Fishing Wharf	(coins)	6	(3 trash)	(fire) (hammer)	Food & Farming. Must be placed on a straight edge of coastline in a navigable location.
Fort	(coins)	–	(4 trash)		Military. Types of Forts are Infantry, Archer and Charioteer
Garden	(coin)	–	(flower)		Municipal: Beautification
Gatehouse	(coins)	–	(2 trash)		Military
Granary	(coins)	12	(3 trash)	(fire) (hammer)	Storage & Distribution

Building	Cost	Employees Needed	Effect on Desirability	Risks	
Hunting Lodge	🪙	6	🗑️🗑️	🔥	Food & Farming
Irrigation Ditch	🪙	–			Food & Farming
Jeweler	🪙	12	🗑️	🔥	Industry
Juggler's School	🪙	5	✿	🔥	Entertainment. Trains jugglers who perform on juggler's stages at Booths, Bandstands and Pavilions.
Library	🪙	30	✿✿	🔥🔨	Education. Needs an initial supply of papyrus to be built and additional supplies of papyrus to continue to function.
Mansion: Dynasty	🪙	–	✿✿✿✿	🔥🔨	Municipal. Must be built on partially on grassland. Stores family savings
Mansion: Family	🪙	–	✿✿✿	🔥🔨	Municipal. Must be built partially on grassland. Stores family savings.

Building	Cost	Employees Needed	Effect on Desirability	Risks	
Mansion, Personal		–	🌸🌸🌸	🔥⚒	**Municipal.** Must be built partially on grassland. Stores family savings.
Mine, Copper		10	🗑🗑🗑🗑	⚒	**Industry: raw materials.** Must be built adjacent to a rocky outcropping marked with metallic nuggets.
Mine, Gemstone		8	🗑🗑🗑🗑	⚒	**Industry: raw materials.** Must be built adjacent to a rocky outcropping
Mine, Gold		12	🗑🗑🗑	⚒	**Industry: raw materials.** Must be built adjacent to a outcropping marked with metallic nuggets
Mortuary		8	🗑	🔥	**Health & Sanitation.** Needs a supply of linen to function.
Palace, City		30	🌸🌸🌸🌸	🔥⚒	**Municipal.** One section must be built on grassland; needed to collect taxes; stores a portion of the city's funds.
Palace, Town		25	🌸🌸🌸🌸	🔥⚒	**Municipal.** One section must be built on grassland; needed to collect taxes; stores a portion of the city's funds.

Building	Cost	Employees Needed	Effect on Desirability	Risks	
Palace, Village	20	🌼🌼🌼	🔥⚒️	**Municipal.** One section must be built on grassland; a city must have a palace before it can collect taxes; stores a portion of the city's funds.
Papyrus Maker	12	🗑️🗑️	🔥	**Industry.** Turns reeds into papyrus.
Pavilion	20	🌼🌼	🔥	Has a musicians' stage, juggler's stage and dancers' stage. Must be placed on intersection
Physician's office	8	🌼	🔥	**Heath & Sanitation**
Plaza	–	🌼		**Municipal: Beautification.** Must be built on paved road.
Police Station	6	🗑️	🔥	**Municipal**
Potter	12	🗑️🗑️	🔥	**Industry.** Turns clay into pottery.
Quarry, Granite	12	🗑️🗑️🗑️	⚒️	**Industry: raw materials.** Must be placed adjacent to a rocky outcropping.

Building	Cost	Employees Needed	Effect on Desirability	Risks	
Quarry, Limestone		12	🗑️🗑️🗑️	🔨	Industry: raw materials. Must be placed adjacent to a rocky outcropping.
Quarry, Plain stone		12	🗑️🗑️🗑️	🔨	Industry: raw materials. Must be placed adjacent to a rocky outcropping.
Quarry, Sandstone		12	🗑️🗑️🗑️	🔨	Industry: raw materials. Must be placed adjacent to a rocky outcropping.
Recruiter		10	🗑️🗑️	🔥🔨	Military
Reed Gatherer		8	🗑️	🔥	Industry: raw material
Road Block		–			Municipal
Scribal School		10	🌸	🔥	Education. Needs papyrus to function.

Building	Cost	Employees Needed	Effect on Desirability	Risks	
Senet House	(barrels)	25	🗑️ 🗑️	🔥 🔨	Entertainment. Needs beer to operate.
Shipwright	(barrels)	20	🗑️ 🗑️ 🗑️ 🗑️	🔥 🔨	Industry. Needs a supply of wood to build and repair ships (except fishing boats).
Shrine	(barrels)	-	🌸	🔨	Religion. Shrines can be dedicated to Osiris, Ra, Ptah, Seth, or Bast
Statue, Large	(barrels)	-	🌸 🌸 🌸		Municipal: Beautification
Statue, Medium	(barrels)	-	🌸 🌸		Municipal: Beautification
Statue, Small	(barrel)	-	🌸		Municipal: Beautification

Building	Cost	Employees Needed	Effect on Desirability	Risks	Control Panel Location/Other
Stonemasons' Guild	(coins)	12	(trash) (trash) (trash)	(hammer)	Industry
Storage Yard	(coins)	6	(trash) (trash)	(fire) (hammer)	Storage & Distribution
Tax Collector	(coins)	6	(flower)	(fire)	Municipal. Cannot colllect taxes unless the city has a Palace; stores a portion of the city's funds.
Temple Complex / Altar / Oracle	(coins) / (coins) / (coins)	50	(flower) (flower) (flower) (flower)	(hammer)	Religion. Only one Temple Complex per city; can be dedicated to Osiris, Ra, Ptah, Seth, or Bast; oracles and altars are dedicated to minor gods.
Temple	(coins)	8	(flower) (flower)	(hammer)	Religion. Can be dedicated to Osiris, Ra, Ptah, Seth, or Bast.

Building	Cost	Employees Needed	Effect on Desirability	Risks	Control Panel Location/Other
Tower	🪙🪙	6	🗑️🗑️🗑️		Military. Gets sentries from the Recruiter's office; built on walls.
Transport Wharf	🪙🪙	5	🗑️	🔥⚒️	Military. Must be placed on a straight edge of coastline in a navigable location.
Wall	🪙	-			Military
Warship Wharf	🪙🪙🪙	15	🗑️🗑️	🔥⚒️	Military. Must be placed on a straight edge of coastline in a navigable location.
Water Lift	🪙	5	🗑️		Food & Farming. Must be placed on straight edge of coastline or adjacent to flood plain.
Water Supply	🪙🪙	5	🌀		Health & Sanitation. Must be placed on grassland.
Weaponsmith	🪙🪙	12	🗑️	🔥	Military. Needs copper to make weapons.

Building	Cost	Employees Needed	Effect on Desirability	Risks	Control Panel Location/Other
Weaver		12			Industry. Needs flax to make linen.
Well		–			Health & Sanitation. Must be placed on grassland.
Wood Cutter		8			Industry: raw materials.
Work Camp		20			Food & Farming

Appendix 2
A Brief History of Egypt

Introduction

First, indulge our compulsion to explain the purpose of this supplement. The culture that we think of when we say "Ancient Egypt" sustained itself for thousands of years. The purpose of this appendix is not to provide a comprehensive history of Ancient Egypt — if we did that, the manual wouldn't fit in the box! Rather, the purpose of this supplement is, first and foremost, to get you excited about this amazing culture. We also want to provide more of a context for *Pharaoh*, so that you can link events in the game with historical fact. Lastly, we want to share some of the themes and ideas that attracted us to this culture. So, without any further ado . . .

Some Quick Geographical Notes

The ancient Egyptians divided their land into two parts, Upper Egypt and Lower Egypt. Upper and lower do not refer to north and south; rather, the terms refer to the flow of the Nile and the elevation of the land. Upper Egypt is the southern region and takes its name because it is closest to the source of the Nile, or up river, and therefore lies on higher terrain. Lower Egypt consists primarily of the Nile delta region and takes its name because it is furthest from the source of the Nile, or down river. It is also closer to sea level than Upper Egypt.

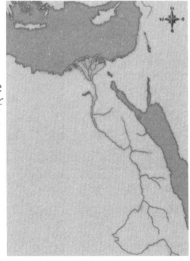

The predominant geographical feature of ancient Egypt was a vast desert bisected by the Nile. The Nile cut a fertile swath along Egypt's length, and the majority of ancient Egyptians lived along the river. The Egyptians referred to the desert as deshret, or the "red land" and called the land along the Nile kemet, or "black land," which is also the name the ancient Egyptians used to refer to their homeland.

Most of Egypt's population lived on the black land along the Nile. Here, they were able to establish farms. The desert, however, was not completely devoid of life. During ancient times, the Egyptians hunted several animal species that thrived among the brush in the desert.

Egypt's particular geography aided its early development. Egypt was naturally protected on three sides. The desert, along with the Mediterranean sea to the north and the Red Sea to the east, provided early Egypt with natural barriers against its foes. Limestone cliffs lining the Nile Valley bolstered the defenses to the east and west. To the south was Nubia, but during Egypt's infancy, the land to south posed no problems.

Without much fear of invasion, Egypt developed the internal infrastructure and economy that led to its longevity. Within a few hundred years of its first unification, Egypt began military conquests abroad and built fortresses to bolster its boundaries. As other cultures developed sea-going vessels, ancient Egypt's natural protections broke down. By this time, however, Egypt had learned to protect itself.

A note about date usage: historians, using papyri and other ancient sources, have been able to reconstruct the chronology of when certain phraraohs ruled and for how long they were in power. There is some debate, however, over when specific pharaohs actually ruled. As a result, dates vary from source to source, and dates used in this supplement might differ from those in other books and articles you've read about ancient Egypt.

One more thing: people have lived along the banks of the Nile for at least 7,500 years. During this incredibly long stretch of time, place names changed. In this text, city names that the ancient Egyptians used are given, followed in parenthesis by their more familiar classical names.

Pre-Dynastic Period
5500-3000BC

The era before pharaohs rose to power is called the Pre-Dynastic Period. Several cultures arose along the fertile banks of the Nile during this time. In Lower Egypt, groups of people lived around Merimda, north of what would become Men-nefer (Memphis). Another culture formed in the Fayuum. To the south in Upper Egypt, cultures formed near Abydos, and several formed at Naqada, or Nubt.

Patron Gods

Religion in Egypt developed regionally. Though in time all the gods were united into one pantheon, most cities stubbornly maintained allegiance to their own regional gods. Some cities held one god in particularly high esteem and viewed that god as its patron. For example, Bubastis' patron god was Bast, Nubt's (Naqada) patron god was Seth, Nehken's (Hierokonopolis) god was Horus, and Abedju's (Abydos) and Busiris' patron god was Osiris.

Different gods rose to prominence at different times, and they often swapped characteristics with one another. For example, one of the earliest pharaohs, Hor-Aha, looked upon Ptah as his patron god. Ptah's stature increased during Hor-Aha's reign, and he became the creator of all the gods. Later, Ra was deemed the creator god and, later still, Amon became the chief god.

Loyalty to a certain patron god occasionally brought mythological overtones to political struggles. At the end of the Archaic Period, Khasekem, firmly united with Horus, battled Peribsen, who affiliated himself with Seth, for rule of Egypt. Interestingly, in Egyptian mythology, Seth is portrayed as a usurper of first Osiris', then of Horus', power. In this instance, no one knows if life is imitating mythology or mythology is imitating life.

Some of these small civilizations exhibited facets of what would become ancient Egyptian culture. By 5500 BC, agriculture became the primary source of food, particularly in southern, or Upper, Egypt. Wheat and barley were grown and stored in granaries of different shapes and sizes. Agrarian communities formed to support the farms.

Burial customs also evolved into a familiar form. The dead were buried in cemeteries on the outskirts of villages, far from the living and away from arable land. Tools and food that they would have used during life were buried along with them. By about 4000 BC, when a second culture had established itself at Naqada, tombs evolved into underground rooms that were supplied with everyday items.

Other conventions practiced by the earliest Egyptians included the use of malachite as eye makeup to reduce the sun's glare and the use of oils for perfume. The throwing stick, used throughout ancient Egyptian history to hunt, was also used during Pre-Dynastic times.

As agrarian communities formed into more organized villages, leaders arose, and certain villages reached dominance. In Upper Egypt, Thinis and Nubt (Naqada), which was associated with Seth, God of Destruction, were the pre-eminent cities. In Lower Egypt, Perwadjyt (Buto) and Behdet (Apollinopolis) were centers of power.

Archaic (Early Dynastic) Period
1st and 2nd Dynasties
3000-2649 BC

It was within the framework of strong regional leaders that ancient Egypt was first unified. Historians disagree on which leader actually united Egypt first. In ancient Egyptian lore, the mythical pharaoh Menes, who hailed from Thinis, is credited with the feat; however, no artifacts found during the time Menes would have lived mention his name.

Most historians are sure that Narmer was one of the first rulers of Egypt, although no one is sure how much of Egypt he ruled. The Narmer Palette, a stone artifact found at Thinis, depicts Narmer wearing the crown of Upper Egypt on one side and Lower Egypt on the other. Some historians point to this palette as clear evidence that Narmer ruled both parts of Egypt.

Historians are certain that Hor-Aha ruled a unified Egypt and founded its first capital at Men-nefer. Hor-Aha selected a site in the middle of Egypt, between the two lands. He called his capital "White Walls," but it would be later referred to as Men-nefer (Memphis). Land for the capital city was created by diverting the flow of the Nile by using a large dike. Hor-Aha also established Ptah as the primary god, and undertook military and trade expeditions to Nubia, Lebanon and Sinai.

Hor-Aha's successors followed his pattern of leadership, and Egyptian culture flourished. Papyrus and hieroglyphics were in use, and the ability to centralize the government was aided significantly by record keeping. The Egyptian government also measured the Nile's inundations and directly managed farm labor. Medical papyri were written, and stone was first used in buildings and sculptures. Nobility were buried in finely decorated mastabas at Abedju (Abydos) and Saqqara.

Several pharaohs followed Hor-Aha, shoring up the union and adding land. At the end of the second dynasty, however, the union broke down. Two men, Persiben and Khasekhem, claimed the throne. Departing from the standard, Persiben took a "Seth name" instead of the traditional "Horus name." In addition to being closely associated with Lower Egypt, Seth, in Egyptian mythology, is Horus' enemy. Khasekhem retained the practice of taking a "Horus Name." During the conflict, Khasekhem was forced southward to Nehken (Hierakopolis), but ultimately managed to defeat Persiben and his forces, reuniting Egypt. After the reunification, Khasekhem took the name Khasekhemwy, which means "two powers have appeared."

By the end of the Archaic Period, Egypt was again unified under one leader. Burial in a great mastaba tomb was the common practice for the nobility. The potter's wheel had been invented, resulting in stronger, longer-lasting ceramic pieces. Trade with neighbors brought needed goods and raw materials into the country. And, due to the conflict between Khasekhemy and Peribsen, Horus was firmly established as the deity of the pharaohs.

Old Kingdom
3rd-6th Dynasties
2649-2195 BC

The Old Kingdom was a time of prosperity in ancient Egypt. Pharaohs firmly united the land with a highly centralized government. Egypt was divided into nomes, each of which was led by a nomarch. Generally, Nomarchs were close relatives of the pharaohs and very loyal to them.

With the union between Upper and Lower Egypt solidified, pharaohs turned their attention to foreign expeditions with the intention of increasing the nation's wealth. Egypt looked primarily to its south for gold and to its east, most notable at Serabit el-Khadim in Sinai, for copper and turquoise. The Egyptians founded settlements in these locations and did battle with Bedouin, Nubians, Syrians, Canaanites and Palestinians. The Egyptians also established settlements in the west at the Bahariya Oasis in the Western Desert. This location was key to facilitating land trade. The expeditions into these areas had the desired effect: Egypt's wealth increased, and pharaohs could afford to spend the country's new-found wealth on massive monuments.

The Old Kingdom also witnessed the rise of the solar cult. The pyramids are in the shape of the benben, where Ra-Atum, the creator god in the solar cult, first appeared. Later in the Old Kingdom, the solar cult became more dominant with the construction of Sun Temples in several cities throughout Egypt.

The Old Kingdom began with the start of the Third Dynasty, and pyramid construction began almost immediately. The second pharaoh of

Pyramid Building

No one is quite sure how the ancient Egyptians built the pyramids. The process is not depicted in any remaining artifacts. Piecing together evidence from the pyramid sites and depictions of the construction of other types of monuments, most archeologists believe that pyramid construction relied on the use of ramps made from unfired mudbrick and wood. Exactly how the ramps were placed in relation to the pyramid remains a mystery. Some think that the ramps were placed perpendicular to the pyramid. As the pyramid grew in size, so too did the ramp. Others think that a series of ramps, each at a 90 degree angle to the previous ramp, circled the pyramid. This would make each ramp shorter, but begs the question of how massive stones were maneuvered around 90 degree turns.

Most agree on how the stones were moved from the quarries to the pyramid sites. Wharves and docks were constructed especially for the pyramid construction, and a ramp leading from the water's edge led to the pyramid site. Stones were pulled on large sledges by potentially hundreds of men. To reduce friction, limestone and water or roller logs were placed under the sledges.

Other theories suspect the use of wind power or simple machines like levers or pulleys to help hoist the huge stones. Of course, there's that silly alien theory, but who really believes that?

the dynasty, Djoser, had the first pyramid built at Saqqara. Imhotep, his vizier who was noted for his intelligence and also served as a high priest for the sun cult at On (Heliopolis), oversaw the construction of the pyramid and acted as its architect. The pyramid, called a "Stepped Pyramid," is essentially six mastabas, one on top of the other, with each level smaller than the previous level. No one is quite sure what the pyramid was intended to portray, but some archeologists suspect that the pyramid was intended to look like a stairway to the heavens.

Several stepped pyramids were built for other pharaohs up until the time of Snofru. Under Snofru, the first pharaoh of the Fourth Dynasty, the pyramid form was perfected. Snofru's first project was to complete his father Huni's pyramid at Meidum. Huni's pyramid began as a stepped pyramid. When Snofru finished the project, he smoothed the sides, foreshadowing the style of pyramids to come.

Snofru began at least three of his own pyramid projects. His first one collapsed under its own weight. His second pyramid, the "Bent Pyramid," is still standing at Dahshur. The angle of the sides changes halfway up, although no one is quite sure why. One theory is that the architects feared another collapse and reduced the angle. Another theory is that Snofru died during the construction, so the angle was reduced to speed up completion. A third theory is that the Bent Pyramid is a gigantic obelisk, designed to represent one of the sun's rays. Regardless, the Bent Pyramid did feature the smooth sides that would distinguish true pyramids from step pyramids.

Snofru's architects finally perfected the true pyramid form with the Red Pyramid. Also located at Dahshur, the pyramid featured the characteristic smooth sides and outer casing of fine stone that subsequent pyramids would mimic. The pyramid takes its name from the color of the monument at sunset.

Pyramid building reached its apex with Khufu's (Cheops') pyramid at Rostja (Giza). The pyramid, the largest still standing, was originally about 476 feet tall with sides of about 750 feet in length. It consists of about 2,300,000 blocks of limestone. The entire pyramid was encased in Tura limestone, brought to the site from On (Heliopolis). Pyramid-building continued throughout the Old Kingdom, and some early Middle Kingdom pharaohs had them built. In all, about 50 royal pyramids have been discovered in Egypt, with dozens of smaller pyramids built for lesser nobility.

The grandeur of the pyramids underscored the pharaohs' standing as gods on earth and reflected the power and wealth they held during the Third and Fourth Dynasties. Some historians estimate that most of the nation's wealth was devoted to pyramid construction.

The Fifth Dynasty marked a shift away from building collosal pyramids. Pyramids were still constructed, but on a much smaller scale, because more resources were devoted to building Temples of the Sun.

Userkaf, the first pharaoh of the Fifth Dyansty, built the first Temple of the Sun at Djedu (Abusir). Six other Fifth Dynasty pharaohs built Temples of the Sun, cementing the solar cult as the central theology.

Eventually, the tightly centralized government that made monument building possible began to break down. While the Fourth Dynasty pharaoh filled government posts with close relatives, the Fifth Dynasty pharaohs did not follow suit. The extensive network of government officials remained, but these posts were no longer filled by relatives of the pharaohs. Rather, nobility from other families filled these posts. From their relationship with pharaoh, they gained power without necessarily having the sense of loyalty that a blood relative might have.

This weakening of the pharaohs' power combined with the

strengthening of that of other families was instrumental in the collapse of the Old Kingdom. The last Old Kingdom ruler, the Sixth Dynasty's Pepy II, governed Egypt for about 94 years, the longest reign of any monarch in recorded history. Age eventually hampered his ability to govern, and the families that had been entrusted to govern the different areas, or Nomes, of Egypt seized more power. Famine completed the downfall of the central government. The climate had changed, and the yearly monsoons that created the Nile's flood ceased. Without the flood, farmland became less fertile until it eventually could no longer support crops. The basis of the economy was gone, people were going hungry, and Pharaoh, a living god on earth, was powerless to do anything. Ancient Egypt again splintered into small communities, each with a provincial leader at its head. The central government disappeared.

First Intermediate Period
7th-11th Dynasties
2195-2066 BC

The First Intermediate Period was a time of strife. Famine's grip on the populace was strong, and leaders of the many small communities did what they could to feed their people. Eventually, Upper Egypt and Lower Egypt again took shape as separate kingdoms.

By about 2160 BC, a group of rulers located at Henen-nesw (Herakleopolis) managed to reunite Lower Egypt. The Herakleopolitan rulers were the rightful heirs to Egypt's throne and claimed full royal titulary. They expelled Libyans and Asiatics who had moved into the Nile Delta looking for food. They repaired old irrigation canals, fortified the borders and opened trade with Byblos in Lebanon. The Herakleopolitan kings were also renowned for their cruelty. Still, they managed to unite

The Nile, the Inundation and the Work Year

Ancient Egyptian civilization would not have developed as it did had it not been for the Nile's yearly floods. Each year, the Nile would flood, or inundate, its banks. The Egyptians referred to this season as Ahket, and during Ahket farming was impossible. Near the end of Ahket, the Nile receded, leaving behind deposits of rich silt that nourished the soil along the banks. Following Ahket was Proyet, or the growing season. During Proyet, farmers would return to the land and plant crops. Reaping was done during Shemu, the last of ancient Egypt's three seasons.

The ancient Egyptians were quick to recognize the value of the Nile's floods. The pharaohs set up nilometers along the river in Upper Egypt to gauge the height of the next flood. Royal priests were entrusted with analyzing the nilometer and issuing a prediction regarding the next flood season.

Disaster struck when the inundation did not occur. The Old Kingdom ended in part due to a series of poor inundations. Crops not only fed Egypt's people, they were the primary currency in which Egypt traded. Without food, famine struck the land and the economy collapsed.

The Nile's flood cycle also contributed to the great monuments and pyramids with which we associate Egypt. Construction on these massive projects took place during the Inundation, when thousands of able-bodied workers would be sitting idly by waiting for the flood to recede. The Egyptian government conscripted the laborers to work on the project, but the workers did reap some benefits. They were paid for their considerable efforts, which supplemented the workers' yearly incomes. It was considered an honor among many to work on the great projects. Helping a pharaoh achieve immortality could go a long way to achieving your own.

The ancient Egyptians, then, had the Nile to thank for almost every aspect of their lives. The Nile provided a relatively reliable source of arable land, and because of it annual flooding created the pool of labor needed to build the lasting monuments to their culture.

disparate people during a difficult time.

Simultaneously, the ruling family from Waset (Thebes) united Upper Egypt, albeit in a much looser confederacy than Lower Egypt. Inyotef I was the first ruler from Waset to begin to unite the territory. He conquered land to the south and assumed the title "Great Chieftain of Upper Egypt." Unlike his Herakleoplitan counterparts, he did not lay claim to the title of Pharaoh.

Inyotef's successors strengthened the confederacy of southern Egypt, and as their power increased, began to call themselves Pharaoh. Once southern nomes had been subdued, they turned their attention northward. Skirmishes along the borders of Upper and Lower Egypt erupted into a full scale civil war.

Mentuhotep II, a descendant of the Inyotefs, emerged and finally defeated the Herakleopolitans. He took the name Sam-towe, which means "unifier of the two lands." He established a new Egyptian capital at Waset.

With a new capital, a new patron god gained influence. Waset's patron god was Amon, and Amon supplanted Ra as the primary god in Egypt. As with Ra previously, Amon was purported to be the original god from whom all other gods sprung. The sun cult remained strong, however, and Amon would eventually become associated with Ra.

In addition to the new dominance of Amon, the First Intermediate Period introduced other changes to religious practices. While Egypt was splintered into its nomes, rulers of villages and regions accorded themselves the same burial rights that had once been reserved for pharaohs and their closest relatives. The Osiris cult also rose in prominence, which further expanded access to burial rights by opening the afterlife to all. Soon, Egyptians from all walks of life entered the afterlife, provided they had enough money to pay for the ritual.

With this pronounced shift in access to funerary services came a marked change in the funerary customs themselves. Pharaohs, as gods, were not judged before entering the afterlife. When the afterlife was opened to mortals, the concepts of a final judgment and last confession were introduced.

Artistically, sculpture and architecture suffered during the First Intermediate Period. Resources were limited, and attention was turned to feeding people and consolidating power. During this time, however, the groundwork was laid for the great literary works of the Middle Kingdom. Without the unifying, religious force of the pharaohs, writers felt freer to express personal thoughts on secular subjects.

Middle Kingdom
11th-14th Dynasties
2066-1650 BC

At the start of the Middle Kingdom, Egypt again recognized pharaoh as the supreme ruler of the land. Conditions had changed considerably from the Old Kingdom, however. The power that regional leaders found during the First Intermediate period continued in the Middle Kingdom, and pharaohs were tasked with keeping their nomarchs under control. Many nomarchs held standing armies, which the pharaohs allowed as long as the nomarchs provided troops when the pharaohs requested them.

After the reunification of Egypt, Mentuhotep II and his successors formed the Eleventh Dynasty and reigned for about 70 years. Military might was strong during their dynasty, and expeditions to Sinai, Palestine, Nubia and Libya were undertaken to both suppress enemies and to take advantage of available natural resources. Mining on the Sinai peninsula and in Nubia again produced the raw materials necessary to make fine art objects.

The Eleventh Dynasty also saw the renewal of trade relations with other countries. Old trade routes were reopened, including the Wadi Hammamat, the dried river bed that served as the link between the Red Sea and Kebet (Coptos). Mentuhotep III also commissioned a trip to distant Pwenet (Punt) to acquire myrrh.

Beer

Ancient Egypt is one of the most studied and revered cultures that has ever existed. What conclusions, then, can be drawn from the Egyptians' passion for beer?

Beer, or heneket in the ancient Egyptian tongue, was the beverage of choice for the ancient Egyptians from the loftiest pharaoh to the lowliest peasant. The beer was fermented from barley, which was most likely baked into a bread at the start of the brewing process. Water was poured over the bread until it fermented, and sometimes it was flavored with fruits. The elixir was passed through a strainer and bottled for consumption.

Beer was drunk through a special mug that had a straw attached to it. At the end of the straw was a filter to remove any of the remaining tidbits of barley bread left in the beer. Beer was enjoyed at home, but the Egyptians also went out to their local taverns to drink with friends and play games.

The importance of drinking beer was recognized at Deir el-Medina, the workers' village established to support the construction work at the Valley of the Kings. In an old attendance record recovered from the sight, spending a day drinking was a legitimate reason for missing work. The ancient Egyptians certainly were an advanced culture.

With the influx of raw materials and the revitalization of the nation's coffers, Egyptian art and architecture again began to flourish. Mentuhotep II built a large mortuary complex carved from a cliff at Djeseru-Djeseru (Deir el-Bahri). Mentuhotep III built many temples throughout southern Egypt, including temples at Abu (Elephantine), Abedju (Abydos) and Waset (Thebes). The temples were decorated with exquisite reliefs and drawings, showing that considerable artistic skill still resided in Egypt in spite of the previous turmoil.

The last action undertaken by the Eleventh Dynasty was an expedition into the Wadi Hammamat to quarry stone for Mentuhotep IV's sarcophagus. The leader of this mining expedition was Amenemhet, Vizier of Upper Egypt. Amenemhet peaceably rose to the throne and became Pharaoh, perhaps illustrating that even provincial rulers can rise to become Pharaoh if they are particularly successful. He started the Twelfth Dynasty, a dynasty that ruled Egypt for over 200 years.

After he came to power, Amenemhet founded a new capital for Egypt. He chose a location in central Egypt about 30 miles south of Memphis and called his new capital Itjawy, or "Seizing the Two Lands." Amenemhat undertook an aggressive campaign to expand Egypt's borders. To the south, he moved well into Nubia as far as the third cataract and established the city of Heh (Semna) where Sesostris III would later build an impressive fortification. Amenemhat also forced the Libyans out of the Fayuum and re-established Egyptian settlements there. Coupled with expansion were new fortifications to protect the borders. The most famous of these fortifications is the Wall of the Prince, a series of fortresses along common inroads to Egypt.

While Amenemhat was away on foreign expeditions, rivals attempted to usurp his throne. As a result, Amenenhat introduced the practice of co-regency, which became one of the keys to the longevity of his dynasty. In the twentieth year of his reign, he named his son and heir, Sesostris, co-regent. They ruled together until Amenemhat's death. With the next pharaoh firmly in power before the current pharaoh's death, pretenders to the throne had a difficult time usurping a pharaoh's power.

The Middle Kingdom also witnessed the expansion of trade relations. Partnerships were established with Syria, Lebanon and Palestine. Aegean artifacts dating to the Middle Kingdom have also been found, indicating trade with Aegean nations directly or through Lebanon.

Monument building in the Twelfth Dynasty shifted away from rock-hewn tombs back to the traditional pyramid. The Twelfth Dynasty pharaohs scattered their pyramids around Egypt. Several built their pyramids at Dahshur, others built theirs outside of Itjawy, and Amenemhat III built his second pyramid at Hawara in the Fayuum. Most of the pyramids were built of mudbrick with Tura limestone casings. One notable exception is Amenemhat III's Black Pyramid. The Black Pyramid was built in part with basalt, lending it its dark color.

Ancient Egyptian literature reached its height during the Twelfth Dynasty. A new canon of texts emerged, and forms included instruction texts and narratives. These texts were quite popular at the scribal schools, and later scribes learned their art by copying the manuscripts over and over. For example, there are four papyri, two drawing boards and about 100 ostraca, or shards of pottery, with *The Satire of the Trades* inscribed upon them. Although the manuscript was written during the Middle Kingdom, all the extant copies date to the New Kingdom, indicating the popularity of the text. It makes sense that *The Satire of the Trades* was appealing to aspiring scribes: it is an instructional text extolling the virtues of being a scribe by humorously criticizing all other trades.

Egyptian theology continued to evolve through the Middle Kingdom. In addition to the emergence of Amon, Osiris continued to gain importance as the God of the Dead. The concept of judgement before entrance into the afterlife had begun during the First Intermediate Period, and Osiris was placed as the last judge during the Middle Kingdom. Pharaohs sought to honor Osiris, and the numbers of fine monuments in Abedju (Abydos), one of Osiris' cities, attests to the god's importance.

The end of the Twelfth Dynasty marked the beginning of the

decline of the Middle Kingdom. Similar to the end of the Old Kingdom, the last pharaoh of the Twelfth Dynasty had an exceptionally long reign. When he died, confusion arose over who was the proper successor. A climate change again compounded the situation. The Nile's floods were exceptionally high and took longer to recede, shortening the growing season.

The situation was not as dire as at the end of the Old Kingdom, but the agricultural difficulties nevertheless weakened the pharaohs' power. The Thirteenth Dynasty, whose pharaohs had moved the capital back to Men-nefer (Memphis), was characterized by dozens of pharaohs with extremely short reigns, indicating the turmoil in the highest government posts. Viziers proved to be more lasting than the pharaohs of the Thirteenth Dynasty, and several served for more than one pharaoh and helped keep the country together.

Without a strong leader, Egypt inevitably fractured into pieces. A new line of pharaohs established themselves at Xois, located in the western portion of the Nile Delta. The pharaohs at Xois ruled at the same time as the pharaohs of the Thirteenth Dynasty.

With this backdrop, the Middle Kingdom closed, and the country again divided into Upper and Lower Kingdoms.

Second Intermediate Period
15th-18th Dynasties
1650-1550 BC

Throughout the Middle Kingdom, immigration increased. People from Asia, particularly the Hyksos, crossed the borders into Egypt and offered their services, often as indentured servants. As time passed, the Hyksos bettered their stature in Egyptian society. When chaos struck at the end of the Middle Kingdom, the Hyksos rose to power.

The Hyksos ruled Lower Egypt and established their capital at Rowarty (Avaris). While they directly ruled only Lower Egypt, they held sway over Upper Egypt as well. The governors of Upper Egypt, based in Waset (Thebes), paid tribute to the Hyksos.

Gods and Goddesses

The Egyptians worshiped dozens of gods and some were more prominent than others (see "Patron Gods" on page 238 for more on the importance of specific gods). Some of the gods belonged to families of gods. The most notable of these sets of gods are the Ogdoad gods and the Eannead gods.

The Ogdoad gods had a cult center in Khmun (Hermopolis) and rose to prominence during the Middle Kingdom. The Ogdoad consisted of god and goddess pairs, each of which governed an aspect of life. The gods were Amon and Amaunet, God and Goddess of Air; Nun and Naunet, God and Goddess of Water; Huh and Hauhet, God and Goddess of Unendingness and Kuk and Kauket, God and Goddess of Darkness. Together, the gods and goddesses were believed to represent the heart of Thoth, the God of All Knowledge. Amon would be singled out as particularly important during the Middle and New Kingdoms and be associated with the earlier god, Ra.

The Eannead is older than the Ogdoad and is populated by some of ancient Egypt's better known gods. Heliopolis was the center of Ogdoad worship. Ra-Atum, the sun god, is the father of the group of gods. His children, to whom he gave birth singlehandedly, were Shu, the God of Air, and Tefnut, the Goddess of World Order. Their children were Isis, Osiris, Nephthys and Seth. Isis and Osiris wed and gave birth to Horus. Ra was eventually thought of separately from Atum and was the primary god throughout the Old Kingdom. Horus was the god of the pharaohs and very closely associated with Ra. Ra, in the morning, was represented as a falcon, and many believed this falcon to be Horus.

Lower Egypt continued to have healthy trade relations under Hyksos rule. Trade routes to Sinai and Palestine remained open, and the Hyksos formed a new trade partnership with the Kush, who had reclaimed land as far north as the first cataract at Abu (Elephantine). The Kush were a distinct nation and culture and established a fine capital at Kerma.

Relations between Upper and Lower Egypt remained friendly enough until Apophis III, an Hyksos ruler, issued an insult to Ta'o II, the leader of Waset (Thebes). In retaliation, Ta'o II invaded the Hyksos' territory and, with the help of Nubian mercenaries, began a war. Ta'o II died in battle, but his son Kamose continued the fight. When he was slain, his brother Ahmose I finished the war, driving the Hyksos back to Asia and once again unifying Egypt under one ruler.

The brief period of Hyksos rule had lasting effects on Egyptian culture. The Hyksos introduced bronze, a much sturdier and versatile metal than copper. This new metal was used in weapons such as daggers and swords. The Hyksos' most famous contribution to Egyptian military technology was the horse-drawn war chariot.

The Hyksos made other contributions as well. They are credited with introducing the upright loom which improved the textile industry; musical instruments such as the lyre, oboe and tambourine; and new foods such as the pomegranate and the olive.

New Kingdom
18th-20th Dynasties
1550-1064 BC

Ahmose began the New Kingdom much as he ended the Second Intermediate Period: with warfare. After forcing the Hyksos out of Egypt, he turned southward to reclaim parts of Nubia. He re-established the capital at Waset (Thebes) and restored the fort in Nubia at Buhen. With the backing of his military, Ahmose also stripped local nomarchs of most of their power, resigning them to mayoralities of cities and villages. Ahmose's military activity set the tone for much of the New Kingdom. Egypt became an imperial force, expanding its borders well into Asia.

This early portion of the Eighteenth Dynasty was not without some internal turmoil. Queen Hatshepsut, Thutmose III's mother, usurped the throne while he has young. She ruled Egypt, assuming all the trappings of a pharaoh, including the ceremonial false beard. Hatshepsut maintained the empire and built many temples and monuments, most notably her mortuary temple at Deir el-Bahri.

Later in the Eighteenth Dynasty, Egypt underwent a radical change. When Amenhotep IV rose to the throne, he changed his name to Akhenaten and introduced monotheism into Egypt. He worshiped the god Aten, who was the God of the Sun's Disk, and established a new capital named Akhetaten. Akhenaten closed down temples to all other gods and confiscated any goods that the temples had on site. He also halted military expeditions to other lands, and much of Egypt's empire was lost during his reign.

While Egypt suffered politically under Akhenaten's rule, the arts blossomed. A new form of portraiture was used in which people, even Pharaoh himself, were portrayed more realistically with physical deformities in full view.

When Akhenaten died, the old theological system was restored and the capital moved back to Waset (Thebes). After the brief rule of several pharaohs (including Tut-ankh-amun), Horemhab, a general in the Egyptian army, assumed the throne. Horemhab restored order within Egypt's borders and set to work reclaiming Egypt's lost land and, prior to his death, named Ramesses I heir to the throne.

The Ramesside period began with Horemhab's death. Ramesses I moved Egypt's capital from Thebes to a new city, Per-Ramesses, near Rowarty (Avaris). Ramesses I's grandson, the familiar Ramesses II (known as "the Great"), conquered new lands and signed new treaties with Asian powers. He also commissioned a large number of construction projects, and his likeness was found in a variety of monuments throughout Egypt.

Ramesses II's military exploits culminated in the Battle of Qadesh, the account of which is the first known detailed report of a major combat engagement. The battle was fought against the Hittites, and it was the first time that Egypt faced an enemy whose power rivaled its own. The Battle of Qadesh could have been disastrous for the Egyptian army. Outnumbered and outmaneuvered, Ramesses II kept his troops' morale high by aggressively charging the enemy. The Egyptian army was spared a crushing defeat when reinforcements arrived. The two sides fought to a draw, and a treaty was drawn up dividing the contested land. Portions of both copies of the treaty survive today.

With New Kingdom imperialism, Egyptians fought many enemies, both known and unknown. In addition to the Hittites, the Mitanni and the Babylonians each rivaled Egypt for control of western Asia. The Sea Peoples, who seemed to have been an amalgamation of several cultures including the Philistines and Minoans, also entered the fray.

While pharaohs led military expeditions, culture at home continued to thrive. The New Kingdom witnessed another shift in burial customs. Because they were plagued by continuous robberies, pyramids as graves were abandoned by pharaohs. Instead, they favored tombs cut into the cliffs of the Valley of the Kings. The Valley of the Kings and the nearby Valley of the Queens, which housed the pharaohs' wives and children, were well hidden from would-be grave robbers. To support the continual construction at the valleys, the village of Deir el-Medina was founded, which housed the craftsmen and laborers who worked in the Valley of the Kings. Much of what we know about the life of the ancient Egyptian commoner comes from artifacts recovered from Deir el-Medina.

The New Kingdom was also marked by a building boom.

Pharaohs commissioned huge temples throughout Egypt. Sculpture, too, was done on a large scale, and several famous examples remain. The Colossi of Memnon, for example, are statues of Amenhotep III that stand 65 feet high.

Art continued to thrive, and artisans began working with faience, a type of glass. They cast the glass to make containers, and used faience for inlays.

After the New Kingdom

The New Kingdom drew to a close at the end of the Twentieth Dynasty. The balance of political power in Asia shifted, and Egypt, plagued with a series of weak pharaohs after Ramesses III, lost much of its land. Libyans to Egypt's west were encroaching more on Egypt's territory, in search of fertile land. Internally, priests of Amun gained more power and eventually usurped the throne.

After tempestuous rule by Libyans and Kushites, the Assyrians invaded Egypt and assumed control. Unlike previous foreign invaders, the Assyrians did not assume the title of pharaoh and considered Egypt to be a province in their empire. The Assyrians, however, were not in power for long. With continued unrest in Asia, Egypt passed through many hands and was led at various times by Babylonians and Persians. An Egyptian, Nectanebo, would briefly rule Egypt, but the country would again fall under foreign leadership.

Alexander the Great seized Egypt in 332 BC, and after his death Ptolemy rose to power. Greeks continued to rule Egypt until the Romans came to power in 30 BC.

Glossary

Some words commonly used when discussing ancient Egypt may be a little unfamiliar. Herewith, a handy glossary:

Amon: the primary deity of the Middle and New Kingdoms. He was originally the God of the Air, but evolved to assume some of the qualities of Ra, the sun god. Amon is also sometimes spelled Amun or Amen.

Akhet: one of the three Egyptian seasons, the Nile's inundation occurred during Akhet.

Ankh: the ancient Egyptian word for life represented by a hieroglyph in the shape of a cross with a loop at the top. When held by deities, the symbol means eternity.

Bedouin: any of a number of nomadic tribes from Sinai that frequently came into contact with Egyptian military.

Canopic Jars: canopic jars held the internal organs of mummified corpses. The jars were entombed with the corpse.

Cartouche: an ellipse that surrounds the name of a royal.

cataracts: the name for the rocky, white water sections of the Nile. Cataracts were important geographical references and frequently were used as a border to divide nations.

corvee: the right of pharaoh to conscript labor for state construction projects.

crook and flail: the symbols of the pharaoh. The crook is associated with the shepherd's staff, and the flail was used to gather resins.

deshret: the Egyptian word for desert, translated as "red land."

faience: a glass-like substance developed by the ancient Egyptians. Faience was used to make some of the most beautiful containers and jewelry.

Fayuum: a region of Egypt that features lakes and tributaries to the Nile. The region was extremely fertile.

Heb Sed: a festival that took place during the 30th year of a pharaoh's reign and every three years thereafter. The festival was designed to reaffirm the pharaoh's ability to rule and featured a ritual run.

Hieratic: a much less complex form of hieroglyphs used for every day writing.

Hittites: one of Egypt's rivals, the Hittites lived in Asia Minor. They were frequent enemies of Egypt, but under Ramesses II rule, Egypt formed an alliance with them.

Hyksos: sometimes called the Asiatics, the Hyksos ruled Lower Egypt for about 100 years during the Second Intermediate Period. During their rule, they introduced new musical instruments and new military accouterments, including the horse-drawn chariot.

inundation: the annual flood of the Nile that refertilized the farmland in its floodplain. Peasants were generally called to work on state projects during the inundation.

Kemet: the ancient Egyptian name for their country; the term means "black land."

Kohl: Egyptian eye makeup that helped protect the eyes from the sun's glare. Kohl is still used today.

Kush: a region of southern Nubia. The Kush had their own distinct culture and established their capital at Kerma. Egypt engaged in trade with the Kush and frequently invaded their territory.

mastaba: an arabic word for bench, mastabas are oblong-shaped tombs used particularly during pre-Dynastic times and the Old Kingdom. Pyramids are believed to have evolved from mastabas.

natron: a type of salt found in the Nile Delta and used during the embalming process to dry the corpse.

Nilometer: a device, usually a pillar of stone or a staircase descending into the river, used to measure the height of the Nile. Nilometers were used to predict the height of the annual inundation.

Nine Bows: a term used first in pre-Dynastic times to refer to conquered enemies. The term was used throughout ancient Egyptian history to refer to enemies of the nation. Traditionally, there were always nine enemies of Egypt, although specific enemies changed over time.

Nome: a province of Egypt led by a Nomarch.

Nubia: the land just south of the first cataract, Nubia's natural resources were very rich. Egypt frequently invaded Nubia, and Nubians were valued as soldiers and police.

Ostraca: shards of stone or pottery that were used to write down notes. Scribes learning their art usually practiced on ostraca.

Proyet: the season of the Egyptian year in which crops were sown.

Pwenet (Punt): a famed land, probably located on the coast of Somalia, Pwenet (Punt) was revered for its fine incense and myrrh. The Egyptians frequently sent trading expeditions there.

Sea People: a group of different Aegean cultures, most likely the Philistines and Minoans, that attacked Egypt during the New Kingdom.

Shabti: a common grave good, shabtis were small statues that served as substitutes in the event that the pharaohs were called to work in the fields or on a construction project during the afterlife.

Shaduf: a water lift used to fill irrigation canals. The shaduf had a bucket on one end and a weight on the other. A peasant would push down on the bucket end, and the counterbalancing weight would help him lift the water out of the river. Some scholars believe that giant shadufs were used to hoist pyramid blocks into place.

Shemu: the Egyptian season of the harvest.

Sidelock of Youth: the hair style that denoted childhood. The head would be shaved except for a single lock of hair on the side of the head. Once a child reached maturity, the lock was shaved off.

Stela: a tablet inscribed with hieroglyphics or reliefs.

Wadi: an Arabic word meaning dry river bed, wadis were often used as roads and were the sites of rich mineral deposits.

YOU SHOULD CAREFULLY READ THE END USER LICENSE AGREEMENT. IF YOU DO NOT AGREE WITH THE TERMS OF THIS AGREEMENT, YOU SHOULDUNINSTALL THE SOFTWARE AND IMMEDIATELY RETURN IT FOR A REFUND FROM YOUR VENDOR OR SIERRA.

This software program, any printed materials, any on-line or electronic documentation, and any and all copies and derivative works of such software program and materials (the "Program") are the copyrighted work of Sierra On-Line, Inc., its parent, subsidiaries, licensors and/or its suppliers. All use of the Program is governed by the terms of the End User License Agreement which is provided upon installation and in the readme file in the Program ("License Agreement"). The Program is solely for use by end users according to the terms of the License Agreement. Any use, reproduction or redistribution of the Program not in accordance with the terms of the License Agreement is expressly prohibited.